BATTLES
OF THE
CIVIL WAR

BY
T. E. VINEYARD

Large Print Edition

Copyright 2014 Large Print Treasury
ISBN-13:978-1496026668
ISBN-10:1496026667

Contents

FIRST BATTLE OF BULL RUN 5

THE BATTLE OF SHILOH 7

THE BATTLES OF FAIR OAKS AND SEVEN PINES............12

THE SEVEN DAYS' BATTLES 15

THE BATTLE OF CEDAR MOUNTAIN 23

SECOND BATTLE OF BULL RUN 25

BATTLE OF ANTIETAM 28

THE BATTLE OF MURFREESBORO 36

THE BATTLE OF FREDERICKSBURG 39

THE BATTLE OF CHANCELLORSVILLE 45

THE SIEGE OF VICKSBURG 50

BATTLE OF GETTYSBURG 54

BATTLE OF CHICKAMAUGA 66

BATTLE OF THE WILDERNESS 72

THE BATTLE OF SPOTTSYLVANIA COURT HOUSE..........76

THE BATTLE OF COLD HARBOR 79

SHERMAN'S MARCH TO THE SEA 82

BATTLE OF CLOYD MOUNTAIN 87

THE SIEGE AND FALL OF PETERSBURG............................90

THE SURRENDER AT APPOMATTOX 95

AUTHOR'S PREFACE

In all history of this American Republic, or perhaps any other nation, there was no conflict that was so terrible as our Civil war. Napoleon's efforts to bring into reality his dream of universal empire would not compare with it.

I have endeavored in this book to describe in detail the chief points that were enacted on the most important battlefields of that War. As those who participated in that War are now fast passing away, and the time will soon be here when they will only be remembered by their deeds of valor on these battlefields, I deem it only fit and proper that those in all walks of life should know more of these battles in detail and of those who participated in them. I think you will get this information from this book, as it is written specially with this view. It should specially appeal to teachers and students who can use it in a supplementary way in connection with the study of history of this period.

I now commend this book to you, and trust that it may be the means of giving you more light on this the greatest civil war of all time, and that it may help to lengthen in the minds of the American people their remembrance of those who participated in it.

FIRST BATTLE OF BULL RUN

At the beginning of July, 1861, the Federals had 30,000 men encamped along the Potomac near the heights of Arlington under the general command of General Winfield Scott, who was a veteran of the war of 1812, as well as the Mexican war, but who was at this time aged and infirm, and remained in Washington, and Brigadier-General Irvin McDowell was in immediate command of the army. Another 20,000 men lay at Martinsburg under General Patterson who like Scott was a veteran of the war of 1812 and of the Mexican war.

At Manassas Junction, about thirty miles from Washington, lay the Confederate army under Brigadier-General Beauregard. General Joseph E. Johnston was in command of 9,000 men in the Shenandoah Valley. Johnston and Beauregard, as well as McDowell, had with Scott and Patterson battled at the gates of Mexico.

General Scott gave orders to McDowell to move against Beauregard and on the 16th day of July the army, with waving banners and lively hopes of victory, and with "On to Richmond" as their battle cry, moved on Manassas. General McDowell brought his army to a halt at Centreville within seven miles of Manassas. Beauregard was apprised of the coming of the Federals. The stream of Bull Run, from which the first great battle of the war derived its name, flowed between the two armies. Patterson failed to detain Johnston in the valley, and General Johnston reached Manassas with his army on the afternoon of the 20th. General Longstreet was also there, who some months later played a distinctive part in the struggle at Gettysburg and in the death grapple of Lee and Grant in the wilderness.

McDowell, after resting his troops for two days at Centreville, thought the time for an engagement was now at hand, so on Sunday, July 21st, at half-past two in the morning, the men were roused for the coming conflict. Their dream of easy victory had already received a rude shock, for on their second day at Centreville a skirmish between two minor divisions of the opposing armies resulted in the defeat of the Union forces with some loss.

Ambrose E. Burnside and William T. Sherman were at this time subordinate officers under General McDowell. Burnside, who figured later in the far more disastrous battle of Fredericksburg, and Sherman, distinguished for his march to the sea.

The Union plan was that General Tyler should lead his division westward and cross Bull Run at the Stone Bridge about four miles from Centreville, and the remainder of the army under Hunter and Heintzelman was to make a circuit of several miles through a dense wood and cross Bull Run at Sudley's Ford. The plan was to attack the Confederate left wing. The march to Sudley's Ford was slower than expected and it was almost noon before this division of the army reached the field near Stone Bridge.

General Tyler early in the day opened fire at Stone Bridge on the Confederates under General Evans, but merely kept up a desultory fire. As the morning wore away the Confederates suddenly discovered clouds of dust rising above the treetops along the Warrenton turnpike, which told them that the main Federal army was on them. Evans quickly turned about and made ready for battle and waited calmly for the approach of the enemy. Presently there was a glimmer of sunlight reflected from burnished steel among the trees and Colonel Burnside led the Federal army from the woods and without delay the battle began and raged furiously.

Meanwhile Generals Beauregard and Johnston were at Manassas, about four miles from the scene of battle, with part of the Confederate army, and had been planning an attack on the Federal left, but on hearing the roar of the cannon and the rattle of the musketry became convinced that the Federals were making their main attack on the Confederate left, and both galloped at full speed to the scene of battle, after leaving orders to the remainder of the army to be brought up to reënforce the small force of Confederates who were trying to hold back the Federals. They arrived on the field at the moment when General Bee's brigade was being driven back. General Bee, in trying to rally his men, called their attention to the fact that Thos. J. Jackson's brigade was standing like a stone wall, and it was here that Jackson won his name of "Stonewall."

The battle raged furiously until 3 o'clock. The chief object was to get possession of Henry's Hill. Beauregard, like McDowell on the other side, led his men in the thickest of the battle. His horse was killed by a bursting shell, but he mounted another and continued. At about 2 o'clock the Confederates were driven from the field and McDowell thought he had won the victory, but General Kirby Smith had arrived from Manassas with the remainder of the Confederate army and was now on the field, after a double-quick march for four miles under a hot July sun. Beauregard determined to make another effort and ordered his troops forward with fresh courage. When the Union army saw the Confederates again approaching, supported by fresh troops, their courage failed and they began to retreat. McDowell tried in vain to rally his men, the Confederates pressed on, the retreat of the Federals became a panic. He again tried to rally his men and make a stand at Centreville but to no avail, the troops refused to listen to his commands. Some of the troops did not stop until they reached Washington, and the first great battle of the Civil war was now over.

The Federal force engaged was about 19,000 men, of which the loss in killed, wounded and missing was about 3,000.

The Confederates had about 18,000 men on the field, and their total loss in killed, wounded and missing was about 2,000. McDowell and Beauregard, the opposing commanders, were old-time friends, having been in the same class at West Point.

It was in this battle that Captain Ricketts was severely wounded and left on the field, and was carried a prisoner to Richmond by the Confederates.

To commemorate the success of the Southern arms at Bull Run the Confederate congress voted a day of Thanksgiving.

THE BATTLE OF SHILOH

Many battles had been fought in America, but they were all skirmishes compared with Shiloh. Napoleon fought but few battles on the Continent of Europe that were more destructive of human life.

In the beginning of April, 1862, General Albert Sidney Johnston was in command of 40,000 Confederate soldiers at Corinth, Miss., about twenty miles from Pittsburgh Landing, on the Tennessee River; the next in command was General Beauregard, who had fought at Bull Run, and had come to reënforce Johnston; General Bragg, of Buena Vista fame, was there, to whom, at Buena Vista, General Taylor had given the famous command, "A little more grape, Captain Bragg." General Leonidas Polk was with Johnston also. He was called the "Fighting Bishop," for he had been a bishop in the church after leaving West Point.

Meanwhile the Union army was gathering at Pittsburgh Landing, under the command of General Grant, and by April 5th numbered 40,000 men. Grant's plan was to attack the Confederates at Corinth, within a few days, and at this time was little expecting an immediate battle, and had left his army in command of his subordinate officers, and on the night of the 5th was some miles down the Tennessee from where his army was encamped.

In the meantime Johnston was moving on the Federals at Pittsburgh Landing, and on the night of April 5th encamped within a mile of the Federal lines.

At the break of day Sunday, April 6th, the Confederate battle-lines moved from the woods on the surrounding hills, and the greatest battle yet fought in the Western Hemisphere was at hand.

General Grant was at breakfast when he heard the roar of the cannon, and made haste by boat to take charge of his army.

General Hardee led the first Confederate attack against the outlying division of the Federals under General Benjamin Prentiss, of West Virginia. Very soon a Confederate attack was made all along the Federal line, led by Bragg, Polk and Breckinridge. A determined stand was made by the Federal division under General W. T. Sherman, but was finally pushed back after inflicting great slaughter to the Confederates. About two and a half miles from the Landing, in a grove of trees, stood a log church, known to the country people as Shiloh, at which they gathered on Sunday to worship, but on this particular Sunday the demon of war reigned supreme, and it goes without saying that the regular service on this fateful Sunday was dispensed with. About this church the battle raged furiously. Near the same was a dense undergrowth, which was held by General Prentiss until late in the afternoon of the 6th, when his entire division was surrounded and compelled to surrender, after repulsing the Confederate attack time after time with great slaughter. This spot has since been known as the "Hornet's Nest."

It was near this place that General Albert Sidney Johnston received his death wound while leading his troops, and in his death the Confederates suffered irreparable loss. He was struck in the leg by a minie ball, and if surgical attention had been given him at once his life would have been saved.

It is the belief of many that the death of Johnston changed the result at Shiloh. Beauregard succeeded to the command and continued the battle. The utter rout of Grant's army was saved only by the gunboats in the river. Beauregard gave orders to suspend operations until morning.

GENERAL ROBERT E. LEE

The Confederates were left in charge of the field on the first day and were in good hope of victory. But ere long their hopes were mingled with fear, for Beauregard had been expecting General Van Dorn with 20,000 men to reënforce him, but he had not arrived. On the other hand, Generals Buell and Wallace arrived during the night with 25,000 fresh troops to reënforce Grant. Everyone knew the battle would be renewed at the dawn of day. At the break of day, April 7th, all was astir on the field of Shiloh, and the dawn was greeted with the roar of the cannon and the rattle of the musketry.

The Confederates were at a great disadvantage as Van Dorn had not arrived, and they were confronted by Grant's overwhelming numbers. Shiloh church was again the storm center, and was used by Beauregard as his headquarters.

During the afternoon Beauregard became convinced that the battle was lost, and ordered a retreat, which was skillfully made, for he maintained a front firing-line, and the Federals did not suspect his retreat for some time.

The Federals were left in possession of the field, while Beauregard's troops were wading through mud on their way to Corinth.

Nothing yet on the American continent had ever been witnessed by any human being that would equal the agony and woe that was endured on this retreat; the road was almost impassable, and the Confederate army, extending along this road for six to eight miles, was struggling along through a downpour of rain, which, ere long, as night hovered over them, turned to hail and sleet. There were wagons loaded with wounded, whose wounds had not yet been attended. The wounded that died on the way were left by the wayside.

Some days after the battle Beauregard reported to his government at Richmond as follows: "This army is more confident of ultimate success than before its encounter with the enemy."

In his address to his soldiers he said: "You have done your duty. Your countrymen are proud of your deeds on the bloody field of Shiloh: Confident of the ultimate result of your valor."

The two days at Shiloh were astonishing to the American people. Bull Run was a skirmish in comparison with Shiloh. The loss on each side was more than 10,000 men. General Grant said that after the battle there was an open field so covered with dead that it would have been possible to walk across it in any direction stepping on dead bodies without the foot touching the ground.

This proved a great victory for the Federals, as it left them in full possession along the Tennessee and in the surrounding country.

THE BATTLES OF FAIR OAKS AND SEVEN PINES

After the battle of Bull Run the Union army was broken up and unorganized. General George B. McClellan was called to Washington to take charge of the army, and in the beginning days of 1862 he found himself in command of 200,000 men. He set about to organize this army and fit them for service. Presently public opinion grew restless, and the North became tired of "All's Quiet Along the Potomac."

About the middle of March McClellan moved a large portion of his army on transports down the Potomac to Fortress Monroe. On April 5th he moved up the Peninsula toward Richmond. He met with a Confederate force under General Magruder near Yorktown, who fell back on Williamsburg as the Union army advanced. At Williamsburg he met a large Confederate force under General J. E. B. Stuart, D. H. Hill and Jubal Early. The Confederates were finally dislodged and forced to retreat by the advance divisions of McClellan's army under Hooker, Kearny and Hancock, who occupied Williamsburg.

The Union army continued their march, and on May 16th reached White House, the ancestral home of the Lees, which is twenty-four miles from Richmond. On every side were fields of grain, and were it not for the presence of 100,000 men, there was the promise of a full harvest.

Great confusion reigned at the Confederate capital on hearing of the advance of McClellan's army. The Confederate army, known as the Army of Northern Virginia, under the command of General Joseph E. Johnston, was arrayed against McClellan's army, known as the Army of the Potomac. And thus was arrayed against each other two of the greatest and best equipped armies that had ever confronted each other on the field of battle. It was now imminent that this would be the beginning of a series of battles between the Army of the Potomac and the Army of Northern Virginia, ending three years thereafter at Appomattox, where the veterans in gray layed down their arms, in honor, to those in blue.

Between these two armies lay the Chickahominy River, which at this time was overflowing its banks on account of recent heavy rains. McClellan ordered his army forward May 20th, and a large division under General Naglee succeeded in crossing the river, and took up a position on the south side of the stream. General McClellan, however, was expecting to be reënforced by McDowell from Fredericksburg with 40,000 men.

General Johnston, discovering the divided condition of McClellan's army, believed that the time had arrived to give battle. At this time "Stonewall" Jackson, with his army, was in the Valley of Virginia, and was seriously threatening Washington. The authorities at Washington deemed it necessary to recall McDowell and thus prevent him from reënforcing McClellan, which proved to be a very serious disappointment to him. McClellan ordered two divisions of his army to advance. One, commanded by General Casey, stationed itself at Fair Oaks farm, and the other, under General Couch, entrenched itself at the cross-roads near Seven Pines, which derives its name from a clump of pine trees, from which the battle fought here derives its name.

No sooner had these positions been taken than they began to entrench themselves and throw out their picket lines, for the advance division of the Confederates could plainly be seen through the timber lines.

On May 30th Johnston gave orders for his army to be ready to advance at daybreak, but during the night a very heavy rain fell and delayed operations until late in the morning of May 31st. About nine o'clock, however, the forces of Longstreet and Hill were ready to move, and advanced rapidly through the woods on the outlying division of the Federals, who made a stubborn defense, driving back the Confederates time after time at the point of the bayonet, and the last time pressing them back to the woods. Here they were met by a furious musketry fire by fresh men from Longstreet's division or infantry. They quickly gave way, and retreated in confusion back to their entrenchments near Fair Oaks farm. Here the Federals took a stubborn stand, but were presently dislodged with great slaughter by an enfilading fire from the brigades of Rains and Rhodes, who had come up on each side.

The Federals fell back to Seven Pines, where Couch's division was stationed. Their situation was growing critical, although they were making a determined stand and had been reënforced by Heintzelman's division. In the meantime Hill had been reënforced by a brigade of Longstreet's division and was making a fierce attack on the Federals. The Confederates were further reënforced by the division of General G. W. Smith. The battle raged furiously until late in the evening, when the Federals fell back a distance of about two miles within their entrenchments along the river.

While this battle was being fought, another at Fair Oaks Station, only a short distance away, was also being fought, in which General Joseph E. Johnston was seriously wounded by a bursting shell, and was carried from the field. He was succeeded in command by General Robert E. Lee, who was afterwards made the commander in chief of all the Southern forces, although the immediate command fell upon G. W. Smith.

Early Sunday morning, June 1st, the battle was renewed and the attack was again made by the Confederates, led by General Smith, supported by Longstreet, but they were pushed back with great slaughter. The Union lines were also broken and a brief lull ensued. Both sides were gathering themselves for another onslaught. Presently the Federals were reënforced by the division of General Hooker. They marched upon the field in double quick time, and were met by a withering artillery fire. Both attacking divisions were ordered forward with fixed bayonets. The Confederates finally gave way and fell back toward Richmond, and the Federals again withdrew to their entrenchment along the river.

It is thought by many that McClellan's failure to follow up the Confederates proved to be the final failure of his Peninsula campaign, for it gave the Confederates time to readjust their army under their new commander.

The forest paths were strewn with the dead and dying. Many of the wounded were compelled to lie in the hot sun for hours before help could reach them. Many of the Federal wounded were placed upon cars and taken across the Chickahominy. The Confederate wounded were carried to Richmond, which was only seven miles away. And many of the Confederate dead at Seven Pines were buried in the Holly Wood cemetery at Richmond, where there are 16,000 Confederate dead. At

Oak Wood cemetery, which is near by, there is another 16,000, which makes 32,000 buried at Richmond.

At this time the defense of Washington was giving McClellan, as well as other Federal authorities, considerable concern, for Jackson with his army had previously taken possession of Winchester and was advancing down the valley. The Federals opposed to Jackson were commanded by Generals Shields and Banks. Jackson made an attack on Shields' army at Kernstown and drove the Federals back, but presently fell back to wait reënforcements under Ewell. The Federals were reënforced by General Fremont. Jackson's activity in the valley caused the president to fear that his goal was Washington. The two armies fought a series of battles in the valley, namely: Front Royal, Strausburg, Newtown and Port Republic, the last-named being the far more important and destructive to life. These were a series of victories for Jackson, for he drove the Federals from place to place, and 3,000 of Banks' men fell into his hands as prisoners. Banks retreated across the Potomac and Jackson joined Lee before Richmond.

Jackson's activity and strategy in the movement of his army surprised both the North and the South. Banks reported to the government at Washington that "Jackson aimed at nothing less than the capture of our entire force."

THE SEVEN DAYS' BATTLES

Early in the summer of 1862, General Lee proceeded to increase his fighting force so as to make it more nearly equal in number to that of McClellan, and to that end every man that could be spared from other sections in the South was called to Richmond. Numerous intrenchments were thrown up along the roads and in the fields about

Richmond, thus giving it the appearance of a fortified camp. General Lee, in an address to his troops, said that the army had made its last retreat.

Each army at this time numbered in the neighborhood of 100,000 men.

Meanwhile, McClellan's army was acclimating itself to a Virginia summer, and now that the sweltering heat of June was coming on, the swamps about their camps were fountains of disease, which began to tell on the health of the men. The hospitals were crowded, and the death rate was appalling.

McClellan proceeded to transfer all his men to the south side of the Chickahominy River, excepting the corps of Franklin and Porter, which were left on the north side of the river to await reënforcements under General McCall, which arrived about the middle of June.

General Lee sent a division of his cavalry, under the command of J. E. B. Stuart, to encircle the army of McClellan. Stuart started in the direction of Fredericksburg June 12th, as if to reënforce Jackson, and the first night bivouacked in the pine woods of Hanover county. Then, turning to the east, he soon came upon a Union force, drawn up in columns of four, ready to dispute the passage of the road, and which fell back in confusion as the Confederates advanced. Stuart pushed on and fell upon a company of Federal infantry at Tunstall's Station, which surrendered at once. The Confederates quickly turned about, crossed the Chickahominy River and joined Lee's army before Richmond, thus giving Lee the desired information of the position of McClellan's army.

Meanwhile, General "Stonewall" Jackson with his army was making haste to join Lee's army, and on June 25th reached Ashland, in striking distance of the Army of the Potomac.

McClellan was pushing his men forward to begin the siege of Richmond. His advance guard was within four miles of the Confederate capital, and his fond hope was that within a few days at most his artillery would be belching forth its sheets of fire and lead into the beleaguered city.

In front of the Union camp was a strip of pine woodland, full of ponds and marshes. The Union soldiers pressed through this thicket, met the Confederate pickets among the trees and drove them back. Upon emerging into the open the Federal troops found it filled with rifle pits, earth works, and redoubts. At once they were met with a steady and incessant fire, which continued nearly all day, and at times almost reached the magnitude of a battle. This is sometimes called the second battle of Fair Oaks, and was the prelude of the Seven Days' battles.

The extreme right of the Union line, under command of General Porter, lay near Mechanicsville, on the Upper Chickahominy. It was strongly entrenched and was almost impregnable to an attack from the front. Before sunrise, June 26th, the Confederates were at the Chickahominy bridge awaiting the arrival of Jackson, but for once Jackson was behind time. The morning hours came and went. Noon came and Jackson had not arrived. About the middle of the afternoon, General A. P. Hill, growing impatient, crossed the river at Meadow bridge, and at Mechanicsville was joined by the divisions of Longstreet and D. H. Hill. Driving the Union outpost to cover, the Confederates swept across the low approach to Beaver Dam Creek through a murderous fire from the batteries on the cliff, but were finally repulsed with severe loss. Later in the afternoon relief was sent Hill, who again attempted to force the Union position at Ellerson's Mill. From across the open fields, and in full view of the defenders of the cliff, the Confederates moved down the slope in full range of the Federal batteries, but the fire was reserved by the Federals. As the approaching columns reached the stream the shells came screaming through the air from every waiting field-piece. Volley after volley of musketry was poured into the ranks of the Southerners. The hillside was soon covered by the victims of the gallant charge. As darkness hovered over them there were no signs of the cessation of the combat. It was nine o'clock when Hill finally drew back his shattered forces to await the coming of the morning. The Forty-fourth Georgia regiment suffered the loss of all of its officers, and thereby was unable to re-form its broken ranks. Both armies now prepared for another day of conflict.

McClellan became convinced that Jackson was really approaching with a large force, and decided to change his base to the James River, leaving Porter with the Fifth corps on the banks of the Chickahominy, to prevent Jackson from interrupting this gigantic movement. It involved marching an army of 100,000 men, with a train of 5,000 heavily loaded wagons, and many siege-guns, together with 3,000 cattle to be driven across the marshy peninsula.

On the night of the 26th, McCall's division was directed to fall back to the bridges across the Chickahominy near Gaines' Mill, and there make a stand, for the purpose of holding back the Confederates. Just before daylight the operations of moving the troops began.

The Confederates were equally alert, and opened a heavy fire upon the retreating columns. The Union force under McCall, by being skillfully handled, succeeded in reaching their new position on the Chickahominy heights, and on the morning of the new day made ready for action. The selection of this ground had been well made; they occupied a series of heights fronted on the west by a cycle shaped stream. The land beyond was an open country, through which a creek meandered sluggishly, and beyond this a densely tangled undergrowth. Around the Union position also were many patches of woods, affording cover for the reserves.

To protect the Federals, trees had been felled along their front, out of which barriers, protected by rails and knapsacks, were erected.

Jackson's forces had united with those of Longstreet and the two Hills, and were advancing with grim determination of victory.

It was two o'clock, on June 28th, when General A. P. Hill swung his division into line for the attack. He was unsupported by the other divisions, which had not yet arrived on the field. His columns moved rapidly toward the Union front, and was met by a hailstorm of lead from Porter's artillery, which sent messages of death to the approaching lines of gray.

The Confederate front recoiled from the incessant outpour of grape, canister and shell. The repulse threw the Confederates into great confusion. Many left the field in disorder. Others threw themselves on the ground to escape the withering fire, while some held their places.

The Federals were reënforced by General Slocum's division of Franklin's corps.

Lee ordered a general attack upon the entire Union front. Reënforcements were brought up to take the place of the shattered regiments. The troops moved forward in the face of a heavy fire and pressed up the hillside against the Union line at fearful sacrifice. It was a death grapple for the mastery of the field.

At this time General Lee observed Hood of Jackson's corps coming down the road bringing his brigade into the fight. Riding forward to meet him, Lee directed that he should try to break the Union line. Hood, in addressing his troops, said that no man should fire until ordered, then started for the Union breastwork 800 yards away. They moved rapidly across the open under a shower of shot and shell. At every step the ranks grew thinner and thinner. They quickened their pace as they passed down the slope and across the creek. Not a shot had they fired. With the wing of death hovering over all, they fixed bayonets and, dashing up the hill into the Federals' line, with a shout they plunged through the felled timber and over the breastworks. The Union line had been pierced and was giving way, and the retreat was threatening to develop into a general rout. But the Federals at this moment were reënforced by the brigades of French and Meagher of Sumner's corps. This stopped the pursuit and, as night was at hand, the Southern soldiers withdrew. The battle of Gaines' Mill was then over.

General Lee believed that McClellan would retreat down the Peninsula, but on June 29th, this being the next day after the battle of Gaines' Mill, he became convinced that the Federals were moving towards the James River. Longstreet and A. P. Hill were again ordered to take up the pursuit of the Federals.

McClellan had left Sumner to guard his retreating columns. Sumner followed up in the rear of the Federals and brought his men to a halt at what is known as the "Peach Orchard," near Savage's Station, and successfully resisted the spirited fire of musketry and artillery of the Confederates. On this same Sunday evening he was attacked by General Magruder with a large force, who was following close on the heels of the Army of the Potomac. Magruder brought his artillery into action, but failed to dislodge the Federals. He then charged the Union breastworks and was met with a vigorous fire, and the battle raged over the entire field. Both sides stood their ground until darkness closed the contest. The battle of Savage's Station was now over. Before midnight Sumner had withdrawn his forces and was following after the wagon trains of McClellan.

The Confederates were pursuing McClellan in two columns, one led by Jackson and the other by Longstreet. The division under Longstreet came upon the Federals at Glendale, where they were guarding the right flank of the retreat. The Federals were attacked by a part of Longstreet's division led by General McCall, but was repulsed with great loss. Longstreet ordered a general attack. One Alabama brigade charged across the field in the face of the Union batteries. The men had to go a distance of 600 yards. The batteries let loose grape and canister, while volley after volley of musketry sent its death-dealing messages among the Southerners. But nothing except grim death itself could check their impetuous charge. Pausing for an instant, they delivered a volley of musketry and attempted to seize the guns. Bayonets were crossed and men engaged in a hand-to-hand struggle. Darkness closed on the fearful scene, yet the fighting continued. The Federals finally withdrew from the field to follow up their retreating columns.

There fell into the hands of the Confederates a field hospital, filled with the wounded, gathered from the fields of Gaines' Mill, Savage's Station and Glendale. These wounded were taken charge of as prisoners, along with their attending physicians. This proved to be a great burden to the Confederates, as they were taxed to their utmost caring for their own wounded.

By this series of engagements McClellan was enabled to reach Malvern Hill, on the James River, with his army intact. By noon on July 1st his last division had reached its position. The Confederates, led by Longstreet, were close on his trail, and were soon brought up to the Union outposts.

GENERAL ULYSSES S. GRANT

Malvern Hill, a plateau a mile and a half long and half a mile wide, with its top bare of woods, commanded a view of the country over which the Confederates must approach. Around the summit of this hill McClellan had placed tier after tier of batteries, arranged like an amphitheater. On the top were placed several heavy siege guns, his left flank being protected by the gunboats in the river. The morning and early afternoon were occupied by several Confederate attacks, sometimes formidable in their nature, but Lee planned for no general move until he could bring up a force which he thought sufficient to attack the strong position of the Federals. The Confederates had orders to advance, when a signal shout was given by the men of Armistead's brigade. The attack was made late in the afternoon by General D. H. Hill, and was gallantly done, but no army could have withstood the fire from the batteries of McClellan as they were massed upon Malvern Hill. All during the evening brigade after brigade tried to force the Union lines. They were forced to breast one of the most devastating storms of lead and canister to which an assaulting army has ever been subjected. The round shot and grape cut through the branches of the trees. Column after column of Southern soldiers rushed upon the death dealing cannon, only to be mowed down. Their thin lines rallied again and again to the charge, but to no avail. McClellan's batteries still hurled their missiles of death. The field below was covered with the dead, as mute pleaders in the cause of peace. The heavy shells from the gunboats on the river shrieked through the timber and great limbs were torn from the trees as they hurtled by. Darkness was falling over the combatants. It was nine o'clock before the guns ceased firing, and only an occasional shot rang out over the gory field of Malvern Hill.

The next day the Confederates, looking up through the drenching rain to where had stood the grim batteries and lines of blue, saw only deserted ramparts. The Federal army had retreated during the night to Harrison's Landing, where it remained until August.

President Lincoln became convinced that the operations from the James River as a base were impracticable, and orders were issued for the army to be withdrawn from the peninsula.

The net result of the Seven Days' Battles was a disappointment to the South, as the Southern public believed that McClellan should not have been allowed to reach the James River with his army intact, although the siege of Richmond had been raised.

Generals McClellan, Jackson, A. P. Hill, G. W. Smith, Joseph E. Johnston and Lee, as well as other commanding officers of this series of battles about Richmond, had been great friends. Some of them had attended school together at West Point, and many of them had enjoyed each other's fellowship while members of the Aztec Club in the City of Mexico, which was an organization of American officers, while for a few months they were in the Mexican capital at the close of the Mexican war. General Franklin Pierce was president of the club, who was afterwards President of the United States.

Generals McClellan and Joseph E. Johnston were special friends even after the war, and in a conversation with McClellan Johnston remarked "You never know what is in a man until you try to lick him."

THE BATTLE OF CEDAR MOUNTAIN

After the failure of McClellan's Peninsula campaign General John Pope was called from the West to Washington to take charge of the Union forces, and arrived in June, 1862. A new army was made up from the respective divisions of McDowell, Banks and Fremont, which was to be known as the Army of Virginia. General Pope at first refused to take command of this army, for the reason that McDowell, Banks and Fremont were superior officers in rank to himself, but was prevailed upon to take the command, which he did, and in an address to his army he ended with the statement, "My headquarters will be in the saddle." When this was shown to General Lee, he grimly commented, "Perhaps his headquarters will be where his hindquarters ought to be."

Fremont refused to serve under Pope, whom he considered his junior, and resigned. His corps was assigned to General Sigel.

Pope's idea was to draw Lee's army away from following that of McClellan down the peninsula, and advanced from Washington with Gordonsville as his objective point. This place, being at the junction of a railroad, was a base of supplies for the Southern army.

The sagacious Lee had divined his intentions and sent Stonewall Jackson and Ewell to occupy this town. Ewell arrived in advance of Jackson, and held the town. Jackson, coming up later, took full command of the army.

On July 27th, A. P. Hill also joined him with his corps, which brought their strength up to about 25,000 men.

The Union army now occupied that portion of the country around Culpeper Court House. Pope soon found that his brilliant success in the West was not like measuring swords with the Confederate generals in Virginia.

On August 6th Pope began his general advance on Gordonsville. Jackson, being informed of his advance, immediately set his army in motion for Culpeper Court House, hoping to crush the Army of Virginia before it reached the neighborhood of Gordonsville, so as to nowise interrupt their base of supplies. Jackson succeeded in crossing the Rapidan River and took a strong position two miles beyond on Cedar Mountain, which is a foothill of the Blue Ridge. From its summit could be seen vast stretches of quiet farm lands, which had borne their annual harvest since the days of the Cavaliers. Its slopes were covered with forests, which merged into waving grain fields and pasture lands, dotted here and there with rural homes. It was on these slopes that one of the most severe short battles of the war was fought.

Jackson placed Ewell's batteries on the slope about 200 feet above the valley, and General Winder took a strong position on the left.

General Pope well knew that the whole North was eagerly watching his movements, and resolved to make an attack, as he must strike somewhere, and do it soon—and here was his chance. He sent Banks, with 8,000 men, to make the attack against the Southerners in their strong position on the mountain side.

Banks advanced against the enemy on the afternoon of August 9th. He advanced through open fields in full range of the Confederate cannon, which presently opened with roar of thunder. The men, heedless of all danger, pressed on up the slope, but were suddenly met by a brigade of Ewell's division, and a brief deadly encounter took place. The Confederate lines began to waver, and no doubt would have been routed but for the timely aid of two brigades which rallied to their support. Meanwhile the Union batteries had been wheeled into position and their roar answered that of the Confederates on the hill. For three hours the battle continued with utmost fury. The fields were strewn with the dead and dying, who fell to rise no more. At length, as the shades of evening were settling over the gory field, Banks began to withdraw his troops, but left 2,000 of his brave men—one-fourth of his whole army—dead or dying along the hillside. The Confederate losses were about 1,300. On account of the peculiar situation of the armies during the battle, their wounded could not be taken charge of, who suffered terribly from thirst and lack of attention as the sultry day gave way to a close, oppressive night. For two days the armies faced each other across the valley, then quietly withdrew.

Pope's first battle, as leader of the Army of Virginia, had resulted in neither victory nor defeat. This battle was a prelude to a far more disastrous battle to be fought a few days later at Bull Run.

SECOND BATTLE OF BULL RUN

The three weeks intervening between the battles of Cedar Mountain and Second Bull Run were spent in heavy skirmishing and getting position for a decisive battle. General Pope's headquarters was at Culpeper Court House, but he had left much of his personal baggage and private papers at Catlett's Station, on the Orange and Alexandria railroad, while his vast store of supplies was at Manassas Junction.

Pope was expecting to be reënforced by McClellan, but they had not yet arrived. Meanwhile Lee had sent Longstreet with his corps to reënforce Jackson, and followed up later himself. Longstreet reached Gordonsville on the 13th day of August.

Lee observed that Pope's position was weak at Culpeper and determined to attack him without delay and gave orders for his army to cross the Rapidan. Pope knew that his position at Culpeper was weak and fell back to a stronger position behind the Rappahannock.

Lee hoped to attack the Army of Virginia before it could be reënforced by McClellan, but, on account of heavy rains, which raised the streams, he was somewhat delayed until Pope had been reënforced by a part of Burnside's corps, under General Reno, and later was also reënforced by Generals Kearny and Reynolds with their divisions of the Army of the Potomac.

Lee sent the dauntless cavalry leader J. E. B. Stuart to make a raid around the Union army. Stuart crossed the Rappahannock with 1,500 mounted men, as bold as himself. After riding all day, and on the night of the 22d, in the midst of a torrential rainstorm, while the darkness was so intense that every man was guided by the tread of his brother horseman, Stuart fell upon the Federals at Catlett's Station, capturing 200 prisoners and scattering the remaining troops in the darkness. He seized Pope's dispatch-book, with his plans and private papers, took several hundred horses and destroyed a large number of wagons loaded with supplies. Among his trophies was a fine uniform cloak and hat, which were the personal belongings of General Pope. These were exchanged later for General Stuart's plumed hat, which he had left behind when surprised by a party of Federals.

Stuart's raid proved a serious misfortune for Pope's army. But Lee had far greater things in store. He resolved to send Jackson to Pope's rear with a large force, Jackson led his army westward, which was shielded by woods and low hills of the Blue Ridge. He passed through a quiet rural community. The majority of the country folk had never seen an army before, though it is true that for many days they had heard the roar of the cannon from the valley of the Rapidan.

General Lee, in the meantime, had kept Longstreet in front of Pope's army to make daily demonstrations, to divert Pope's attention from Jackson's movements and lead him to believe that he was to be attacked in front.

Jackson suddenly, on August 26th, emerged from the Bull Run Mountains and marshaled his clans on the plains of Manassas.

Pope was astonished to find Jackson in his rear, and hastened with all speed with his forces toward Manassas Junction, where he had vast stores of provisions and munitions of war, but he was too late to save them. They had been taken by General Stuart in advance of Jackson's army. This was a serious loss to Pope. The spoils of the capture were great, including 300 prisoners, 125 horses, ten locomotives, seven long trains of provisions, and vast stores and munitions of war. Pope was moving against Jackson with a far larger army, and was expecting to be reënforced from the Army of the Potomac, while on the other hand, Longstreet was hastening to reënforce Jackson, but had not arrived.

Pope, hoping to crush Jackson's army before he could be reënforced by Longstreet, sent a force to interpose Longstreet at Thoughfare Gap. Jackson was not to be caught in a trap. He moved from Manassas Junction to the old battlefield of Bull Run.

Late in the afternoon of the 29th he encountered King's division of McDowell's corps, near the village of Groveton, and a sharp fight was opened and kept up until after dark.

On the following day, August 29th, the first day's battle was fought. Pope was still hopeful of crushing Jackson's army before the arrival of Longstreet, and ordered a general advance across Bull Run.

Ere long a loud shout arose from Jackson's men that told too well of the arrival of Longstreet. Far away on the hills could be seen the marching columns of Longstreet, who had passed through the gap in safety and was now rushing upon the field. Pope had lost the opportunity of fighting the army of his opponent in sections.

The field was almost the same that the opposing armies had occupied the year before, when the first great battle of the war was fought, and many of them were the same men.

The two armies faced each other in a line five miles long. Late in the afternoon, the regiments, under Kearny and Hooker, charged the Confederate left, which was swept back and rolled upon the center. But presently General Hood, with his famous Texan brigade, rushed forward in a wild, irresistible dash, pressed the Federals back and captured several prisoners.

Darkness closed over the scene and the two armies rested on their arms until morning.

Over the gory field lay multitudes of men who would dream of battlefields no more.

Lee and Pope each believed that the other would withdraw his army during the night, and each was surprised in the morning to find his opponent on the field. It was quite certain that on this day, August

30th, there would be a decisive battle, in which one army would be victor and the other defeated. Both armies were in full force, the Confederates with over 50,000 men, whose left wing was commanded by Jackson and the right by Longstreet, and the Union army with about 65,000 men, whose left wing was commanded by Porter and the right by Keno.

In the early hours of the morning the hills echoed with the firing of artillery. Porter made an infantry attack in the forenoon, and was pressed back in great confusion by superior numbers. One attack after another followed. In the afternoon a large part of the Union army made a desperate attack on the Confederate left, under Jackson, but their lines were swept by an enfilading fire from the batteries of Longstreet. Ghastly gaps were cut in the Federal ranks, and they fell back, but rallied again and again to the attack, each time to be mowed down by Longstreet's artillery. At length Longstreet's whole line rushed forward and the Union front began to waver. General Lee ordered a general advance. Pope retreated across Bull Run, leaving several thousand prisoners in the hands of the Confederates.

Pope led his army back to the entrenchments at Washington, while Jackson and Stuart followed close on the heels of his army, and he was compelled to make several stands in battle on his retreat, in one of which General Kearny was killed.

BATTLE OF ANTIETAM

After Pope's disastrous defeat at Second Bull Run he begged to be relieved of the command of the army. He gave as one of the causes of his defeat that General Fitz John Porter had disobeyed orders. General Porter's explanation to the Court Marshal failed to convince it and he was dismissed from the service.

The Army of Virginia and that of the Potomac being united, the command was handed to the "Little Napoleon" of Peninsula fame, George B. McClellan.

The South was overjoyed with its victory at Bull Run—twice it had unfurled its banner in triumph on this battlefield—twice its army had stood on the road that leads to Washington, only by some strange destiny of war to fail to enter it on the wave of victory.

This subject, "The Battle of Antietam," is considered one of the turning points of the war, for it was after this battle that President Lincoln issued his emancipation proclamation, although it is said that he had it prepared for some time but on account of the continued defeat of his armies in Virginia he could not see his way clear to declare it until after the battle of Antietam.

Lee's army, 50,000 strong, crossed the Potomac and concentrated around Frederick, Md., only about forty miles from Washington. When it became known that Lee was advancing into Maryland and was threatening Washington, McClellan pushed his forces forward to encounter the invaders. The people of the vicinity, and even at Harrisburg, Baltimore and Philadelphia, were filled with consternation. Their fear was intensified by the memory of Second Bull Run, a few weeks before, and by the fact that at this time General Bragg was marching northward across Kentucky with a great army, threatening Louisville and Cincinnati.

Lee sent Jackson against the Union forces at Harper's Ferry, which is at the junction of the Potomac and Shenandoah Rivers, at which place there were stored valuable stores and munitions of war. This place was made famous by John Brown's raid a few years before.

Jackson reached the neighborhood of Harper's Ferry on the morning of the 13th, and captured the town with but little opposition on the morning of the 15th. There were turned over to him 11,500 prisoners, seventy-three guns, 13,000 small arms, 200 wagons, and a large store of supplies. In this enterprise Lee had achieved an important and valuable success.

Longstreet, who had advanced to Hagerstown, probably with the intention of invading Pennsylvania, was hastily recalled and sent to reënforce D. H. Hill, who was being severely pushed at Boonsborough Gap by McClellan. The defense of this path had been very necessary to Lee, but, after a desperate conflict, the Union army succeeded in forcing its way through, this being the first set-back to Lee's invasion, and he conceived at once that a great battle was at hand and began to concentrate his forces.

Jackson was marching with all haste to Sharpsburg, near by Antietam Creek, having left A. P. Hill to receive the surrender at Harper's Ferry, and on the morning of the 16th the whole army, with the exception of the force of A. P. Hill, left at Harper's Ferry, was concentrated behind Antietam Creek.

McClellan's army reached the opposite side of the stream on the same day.

The bulk of the Confederate forces, under Longstreet and D. H. Hill, stood along the range of heights between Sharpsburg and Antietam Creek, with Longstreet on the right and Hill on the left, and Hood's division on the Hagerstown road north of Miller's farm, and near that point, in the rear, Jackson's exhausted troops were in reserve.

His lines, stretching from the Hagerstown road towards the Potomac, were protected by Stuart's cavalry. General Lee had his headquarters in a tent on a hill near Sharpsburg, where the National Cemetery now is, and from that point he overlooked much of the country that was made a battlefield the next day.

Antietam Creek was spanned by four stone bridges, which were strongly guarded.

McClellan made his headquarters at the fine brick mansion of Philip Pry, about two miles east of Antietam. His army was posted in front on each side, one wing under Sumner and the other under Hooker. Farther down the stream, and not far from bridge No. 3, Burnside's corps was posted. McClellan's artillery was planted on the hills in front of Sumner and Hooker. This was the general position of the contending armies on the 16th.

This was a day of intense anxiety and unrest in the valley of the Antietam. The people, who had lived in the farm houses that dotted the golden autumn landscape in this hitherto quiet community, had now abandoned their homes and given place to the gathering thousands who were marching to the stern command of the officers. It was a day of maneuvering and getting position preparatory to the coming mighty conflict.

The two great armies now lay facing each other in a grand double line three miles in length. At one point they were so near together that the pickets could hear each other tread. It would require no prophet to foretell what would happen on the morrow.

On the night of the 16th few officers found relief from anxiety, and it goes without saying that many a soldier on this particular night, with his mind on the battle which was to be fought on the morrow, did not close his eyes in slumber.

Beautiful and clear the morning broke over the Maryland hills on the fateful 17th of September, 1862. The sunlight had not yet touched the crowned hilltops when artillery fire announced the opening of the battle. The contest was opened by Hooker with about 8,000 men. He made a vigorous attack on the Confederate left, commanded by Jackson, and was supported by Doubleday on the right, and Meade on the left. He had not gone far before the glint of the rising sun disclosed the bayonet points of a large Confederate force standing in a cornfield in his immediate front. This was a part of Jackson's corps, who had arrived during the morning of the 16th from the capture of Harper's Ferry, and had been posted in this position to surprise Hooker in his advance. The outcome was a terrible surprise to the Confederates. Hooker's batteries hurried into action and opened with canister on the cornfield. Hooker's object was to push the Confederates back through a line of woods and seize the Hagerstown road and the woods beyond in the vicinity of the Dunker church. Around this church on this fateful day the demon of war reigned supreme, and near this church stood the fine mansion of a Mr. Mumma, which was fired by a retreating column of Confederate troops and burned throughout the entire engagement. The Federal batteries on the east side of the Antietam poured an enfilading fire on Jackson that galled him very much. The Confederates stood bravely against this fire and made a determined resistance. Back, and still further back, were Jackson's men driven across the field, every stalk of corn in which was cut down by the shot and shell as closely as a knife could have done it. On the ground the fallen lay in rows, precisely as they had stood in the ranks. The Confederates were driven from the cornfield into a patch of woods. Hooker now advanced his center under Meade to seize the Hagerstown road and the woods beyond. They were met by a murderous fire from Jackson, who had just been reënforced by Hood's refreshed troops, who fell heavily upon Meade in the cornfield. Hooker called upon Doubleday for aid, and a brigade was forwarded at double-quick across the cornfield in the face of a terrible storm of shot and shell. The Federals were further reënforced by Mansfield's corps, and while his divisions were deploying this veteran commander was mortally wounded. General Williams succeeded to the command of his corps, who pushed on across the open fields and seized a part of the woods on the Hagerstown road. At the same time Greene's division took position to the left of the Dunker church. This was on high ground and was the key to the Confederate left wing. But Greene's troops were exposed to a galling fire from the division of D. H. Hill and he called for reënforcements. General Sumner sent Sedgwick's division across the creek to reënforce Greene. His troops advanced straight towards the conflict. They found General Hooker severely wounded in the foot, which became so painful that he was carried off the field and left his troops in the command of Sumner. A sharp artillery fire was turned on Sedgwick before he reached the woods, west of the Hagerstown Pike, but once in the shelter of the thick trees he passed in safety to the western edge. Here the division found itself in an ambush.

The Confederates had been heavily reënforced by several brigades under Walker and McLaws, having just arrived from Harper's Ferry, and had not only blocked the front but had worked around to the rear of Sedgwick, who was wounded in the awful slaughter that followed, but he and Sumner finally extricated their men after severe loss. The Federals were now reënforced by Franklin's fresh troops and were able to hold the cornfield and part of the woods over which the conflict had raged till the ground was saturated with blood.

Sedgwick was twice wounded and carried from the field. The command of his division involved on General Howard.

It was now about noon and the battle had been raging since early in the morning. Another deadly conflict was in progress near the center. Sumner's corps had crossed the stream and made a desperate assault on the Confederates under D. H. Hill, stationed to the south of where the battle had previously raged and along a sunken road, since known as "Bloody Lane." The fighting here was of a most desperate character and continued nearly four hours. The Federal advance was led by Generals French and Richardson, who captured a few flags and several prisoners, but failed to carry the heights along which the Confederates were posted. Richardson was mortally wounded while leading a charge and was succeeded by General Hancock, but his men finally captured Bloody Lane with the 300 living men who remained to defend it.

The final Federal charge was made at this point by Colonel Barlow, who displayed the utmost bravery, where he won a brigadier-generalship. He was later wounded and carried off the field. The Confederates had fought desperately to hold their position at Bloody Lane, and when it was captured it was filled with dead bodies. It was now after one o'clock and the firing ceased for the day on the Union right and center.

General Burnside was in command of the Federal left wing and had remained inactive for some hours after the battle had begun at the other end of the line, having finally received orders from McClellan to cross the stone bridge, since known as Burnside's Bridge, and drive the Confederates out of their strong position. The Confederates at this bridge were commanded by General Toombs, who had orders from General Lee to hold the bridge at all hazards. They were behind strong breastworks and rifle pits, which commanded the bridge with both a direct and enfilading fire. General Robert Toombs had been a former United States senator and a member of Jefferson Davis' cabinet. Perhaps the most notable event of his life was the holding of the

Burnside Bridge at Antietam for three hours against the fearful onslaughts of the Federals. Burnside's chief officer at this time was General Jacob D. Cox, afterwards governor of Ohio, who succeeded General Reno, killed at South Mountain or Boonsborough Gap. On General Cox fell the task of capturing the stone bridge.

The Confederates had been weakened at this point by the sending of Walker to the support of Jackson, where, as we have noticed, he took part in the deadly assault upon Sedgwick's division.

Toombs, with his small force, had a hard task of defending the bridge, notwithstanding his advantage of position. McClellan sent several urgent orders to General Burnside to cross the bridge at all hazards. Burnside forwarded these to Cox and in the fear that the latter would not be able to carry the bridge by a direct front attack, he sent General Rodman with a division to cross the creek at a ford below. This was accomplished after much difficulty. One assault after another was made upon the bridge in rapid succession, which was at length carried at the cost of 500 men. Burnside charged up the hill and drove the Confederates almost to Sharpsburg. The fighting along the Sharpsburg road might have resulted in the Confederates' disaster and the capture of General Lee's headquarters had it not been for the timely arrival of A. P. Hill's division, which emerged out of a cloud of dust on the Harper's Ferry road and came upon the field at double quick, and, under a heavy fire of artillery, charged upon Burnside's columns and after severe fighting, in which General Rodman was mortally wounded, drove the Federals back almost to the bridge. The pursuit was checked by the Federal artillery on the eastern side of the stream. Darkness closed the conflict.

Lee had counted on the arrival of A. P. Hill in time to help hold the Federals in check at the bridge, but he was late and came up just in time to save the army from disastrous defeat.

With the gloom of that night ended the conflict known as Antietam.

For fourteen hours more than 100,000 men, with 500 pieces of artillery, had engaged in Titanic conflict. As the battle's smoke rose and cleared away the scene presented was one to make the stoutest heart shudder. There lay upon the ground, scattered for three miles over the valleys and hills, and in the improvised hospitals, more than 20,000 men.

Horace Greeley was probably right when he said that this was the bloodiest day in American history.

THE BATTLE OF MURFREESBORO

The fall months of 1862 had been spent by Generals Bragg and Buell in racing across Kentucky, each at the head of a large army. Buell had saved Louisville from the hands of the Confederates, while on the other hand Bragg had succeeded in carrying away a large amount of plunder and supplies for his army which he had gathered from the country through which he passed, and of which his army was in great need.

The authorities at Washington became impatient with Buell on account of his permitting the Confederate army to escape intact, and decided to relieve him of the command of the army, which was handed to General W. S. Rosecrans, who had won considerable distinction by his victories at Corinth and other engagements in the West. The Union army was now designated as the Army of the Cumberland.

Bragg was concentrating his army at Murfreesboro, in central Tennessee, which was near Stone's River, a tributary of the Cumberland River.

On the last days of December General Bragg was advised of the Federals' advance from Nashville, which is about thirty miles from Murfreesboro, and he lost no time in taking position and getting his army into well-drawn battle lines. His left wing under General Hardee, the center Polk, and his right wing under Breckenridge, his cavalry division was commanded by Generals Wheeler, Forrest and Morgan. His lines were three miles in length. On December 30th the Federals came up from Nashville and took position directly opposite in a parallel line. The Federal left was commanded by Thos. L. Crittenden, whose brother was a commander in the Confederate army, and were sons of a famous United States senator from Kentucky. The Federal center was in command of General George H. Thomas, and the right wing under General McCook. Rosecrans had under his command about 43,000 men, while the strength of the Confederates was about 38,000.

The two armies bivouacked within musket range of each other, and the camp-fires of each were clearly seen by the other, as they shown through the groves of trees.

It was plain to be seen that a deadly combat would begin with the coming of the morning.

Rosecrans had planned to attack the Confederate right under Breckinridge, while on the other hand Bragg had planned to attack the Federal left under McCook, and to seize the Nashville turnpike and thereby cut off Rosecrans' retreat. Neither, of course, knew of the other's plan.

At the break of day, on December 31st, the Confederate left moved forward in a magnificent battle-line, about a mile in length and two columns deep. At the same time the Confederate artillery opened with their cannon. The Federals were astonished at so fierce and sudden a charge and were ill prepared. Before McCook could arrange them several batteries were overpowered and several heavy guns fell into the hands of the Confederates. The Union troops fell back in confusion and seemed to have no power to check the impetuous charge of the onrushing foe. Only one division, under General Philip H. Sheridan, held its ground. Sill's brigade of Sheridan's division drove the Confederates in front of its back to their entrenchments, but in this charge the brave commander lost his life.

While the battle raged with tremendous fury on the Union right, Rosecrans was three miles away, throwing his left across the river. Hearing the terrific roar of the cannon and rattle of the musketry, he hastened to attack Breckinridge, hoping to draw a portion of the Confederate force away from the attack on his right. Ere long the sound of battle was coming nearer, and he rightly divined that his right wing was being rapidly driven upon his center by the dashing soldiers of the South. He ordered McCook to dispute every inch of the ground; but McCook's command was torn to pieces except the division of Sheridan, which stood firm against the overwhelming numbers, which stand attracted the attention of the country and brought military fame to Sheridan. He checked the onrushing foe at the point of the bayonet, and re-formed his lines under a heavy fire. Rosecrans ordered up the reserves to the support of the Union center and right. Here for two hours longer the battle raged with unabated fury. Three times the Confederate left and center were thrown against the Union lines, but failed to break them. At length it was discovered that the ammunition was exhausted in Sheridan's division and he withdrew in good order to a plain near the Nashville road. The Confederates' advance was checked by the division of Thomas.

It was now in the afternoon, and still the battle raged in the woods and on the hills about Murfreesboro.

The Federal right and center had been forced back to Stone's River, while Bragg's right was on the same stream close to the Federal line.

In the meantime Rosecrans had massed his artillery on a hill overlooking the field. He had also re-formed his broken lines, and had called 12,000 fresh troops from his left into action. The battle re-opened with utmost fury, and the ranks of both armies were torn with grape and canister and bursting shells.

General Breckinridge brought all of his division excepting one brigade into the action. They had for some time been inactive and were refreshed by a short rest. The Confederates now began a vigorous attack upon the Federal columns, but were swept by a raking artillery fire. They rallied again to the attack, but their ranks were again swept by Rosecrans' artillery and the assault was abandoned.

Darkness was now drawing over the scene of battle, and the firing abated slowly and died away. It had been a bloody day, the dead and dying lay upon the field and in the hospitals in great numbers, and with the awful gloom and suffering of that night ended the first day's battle at Murfreesboro.

The next day was the first of the new year, and both armies remained inactive during the entire day, except to quietly prepare to renew the conflict on the morrow. The renewal of the battle on January 2d was fully expected, but there was but little fighting until late in the afternoon. Rosecrans had sent General Van Cleve across the river to occupy an elevation from which he could shell the town of Murfreesboro.

Bragg sent Breckinridge to dislodge this division, which he did with splendid effect. But Breckinridge's men became exposed to the raking fire of the Federal artillery across the stream and retreated to a place of safety with a loss of 1,700 men killed and wounded.

The next day brought no further conflict. On the night of January 3d General Bragg began to move his army away to winter quarters at Shelbyville.

Murfreesboro was one of the great battles of the war, and, except at Antietam, had not thus far been surpassed. The losses were about 13,000 to the Federals, and about 10,000 to the Confederates. Both sides claimed the victory—the South because of Bragg's decided success on the first day; the North because of Breckinridge's fearful repulse on the last day's battle, and of Bragg's retiring in the night and refusing to fight again.

THE BATTLE OF FREDERICKSBURG

The silent city of military graves at Fredericksburg is a memorial of one of the bloodiest battles of the war. General McClellan failed to follow up the retreating Southern army after the battle of Antietam, and thereby lost favor with the authorities at Washington, and was relieved of the command of the army, which was handed to General Ambrose E. Burnside, who took command of the Army of the Potomac on November 9, 1862, and on the following day McClellan took leave of his troops.

Burnside changed the whole plan of the campaign and decided to move on Fredericksburg on the Rappahannock River. His army moved forward in three divisions, under Sumner, Hooker and Franklin. They were delayed several days in crossing the river, due to the failure of the arrival of the pontoon bridges. A council of war was held on the night of December 10th, in which the officers were opposed to the plan of battle, but Burnside was determined to carry out his original plan immediately. After two days of skirmishing with the Confederate sharpshooters he succeeded in getting his army across the river on the morning of December 13th.

General Lee had by this time entrenched his army on the hills surrounding Fredericksburg. His line stretched for five miles along the range of hills, surrounding the town on all sides save the east, where the river flows. The strongest position of the Confederates was on Marye's Heights, in the rear of the town. Along the foot of this hill was a stone wall about four feet high, bounding the eastern side of the Telegraph road, being depressed a few feet below the surface of the stone wall, and thus it formed a breastwork for the Confederate troops. Behind this wall a strong Confederate force was concealed, while higher up the hill in several ranks the main army was posted. The right wing of the Confederate army, consisting of about 30,000 men, commanded by "Stonewall" Jackson, was posted on an elevation near Hamilton's crossing of the Fredericksburg and Potomac railroad. The left wing was posted on Marye's Heights, and was commanded by the redoubtable Longstreet. The Southern forces numbered about 75,000 men.

The town proper and the adjoining valleys had been occupied for two days by the Federal troops, marching to and fro and making ready for a decisive conflict, which required no prophet to foretell was near at hand. Franklin's division of 40,000 men was strengthened by a part of Hooker's division and was ordered to make the first attack on the Confederate right, under Jackson. Sumner's division was also reënforced from Hooker's division and was formed for an assault against the Confederates, posted on Marye's Heights.

From the position taken by the Confederate forces their cannons and field artillery poured shot and shell into the town of Fredericksburg. Every house became a target, though deserted except by a few venturesome riflemen. There was scarcely a house that escaped. Ruined, battered and bloody Fredericksburg three times was a Federal hospital and its back yards became little cemeteries.

All this magnificent battle formation had been effected under cover of a dense fog, and when it lifted on that fateful Saturday there was revealed a scene of truly military grandeur. Concealed by the curtain of nature, the Southern army had entrenched itself most advantageously upon the hills, and the Union force massed in strength below, lay within cannon shot of their foe. The Union army totaled 113,000 men.

When the fog lifted in the forenoon of December 13th, Franklin's division was revealed in full strength marching and counter-marching in preparation of the coming conflict. Officers in new uniforms, thousands of bayonets gleaming in the sunshine, champing steeds, rattling gun-carriages whisking artillery into proper range, formed a scene of magnificent grandeur, which excited the admiration of all, even the Confederates. This maneuver has been called the grandest military scene of the war, yet after all this show, Burnside's subordinate officers were unanimous in their belief in the rashness of the undertaking. It is said by historians that the Army of the Potomac never went down to battle with less alacrity than on this day at Fredericksburg.

The advance began about the middle of the forenoon on Jackson's right, which was made by the divisions led by Generals Meade, Doubleday and Gibbon, who endeavored to seize one of the opposing heights on Jackson's extreme right. The advance was made in three lines of battle, which were guarded in front and on each flank by Jackson, whose artillery swept the field by both a front and an enfilading fire as the attacking columns advanced. And as the divisions approached within range Jackson's left poured a deadly fire of musketry upon them, which mowed down brave men in the Union lines in swaths, leaving broad gaps where men had stood.

On the Federal columns came, only to be swept again and again by this murderous fire, but were at length repulsed.

The Confederate lines were broken only once by a part of Meade's division, which captured a few flags and several prisoners. The lost ground was soon recovered by the Confederates. Some of the charges made by the Federals in this engagement were heroic in the extreme. In one advance knapsacks were unslung and bayonets fixed; a brigade marched across a plowed field and passed through broken lines of other brigades, which were retiring in confusion from the leaden storm. In every instance the Federals were driven back in shattered columns.

The dead and wounded lay in heaps. Soldiers were fleeing and officers were galloping to and fro, urging their lines forward.

At length they received orders to retreat, and in retiring from the field the destruction was almost as great as during the assault. Most of the wounded were brought from the field after the engagement, but the dead were left where they fell.

During this engagement General George D. Bayard was mortally wounded by a shot that had severed the sword-belt of a subordinate officer who was standing by.

While Franklin's division was engaged with the Confederate right, Sumner's division was engaged in a terrific assault upon the works of Marye's Heights, which was the stronghold of the Confederate forces. Their position was almost impregnable, consisting of earthworks, wood and stone barricades, running along the sunken road near the foot of the hill. The Federals were not apprised of the sunken road nor of the Confederate force concealed behind the stone wall, under General Cobb. When the Federals advanced up the road they were harassed by shot and shell at every step, but came dashing on in line notwithstanding the terrific fire which poured upon them. The Irish brigade of Hancock's division, under General Meagher, made a wonderful charge, the Irish soldiers moved steadily up the ridge until within a few yards of the sunken road, from which the unexpected fire mowed them down. When they returned from the assault but 250 out of 1,200 men reported under arms from the field, and all these were needed to care for their wounded comrades. This brigade, as we will notice later, distinguished itself at Gettysburg and other engagements. It lost more men in killed and wounded than any regiment that left the State of New York. When returning to be mustered out in 1865, it had only forty-seven men out of 950 that enlisted four years before on first leaving for the front.

Sumner sent column after column against this strong position, but they were repulsed with great slaughter. The approach was completely commanded by the Confederate batteries.

Not only was the Confederate fire disastrous upon the approaching columns, but it also inflicted great damage upon the masses of the Federal army, and it is said that in front of Marye's house, which was in the center where the charge was made, the Federals fell three deep in one of the bravest and bloodiest charges of the war.

Six times did the Federals, raked by the deadly fire of Washington's artillery, advance to within 100 yards of the sunken road, only to be driven back by the rapid fire of the Confederate infantry concealed there. The Confederates' effective and successful work in this battle was not alone due to their strong position, but also to the skill and generalship of the leaders, and the courage and well-directed aim of their cannoneers and infantry.

The whole plain was covered with men, the living men running here and there, their broken lines closing up and the wounded being carried to the rear.

The point and method of attack made by Sumner was anticipated by the Confederates, and careful preparation had been made to meet it.

As the Federal columns advanced without hurrah or battle-cry, their entire lines were swept by a heavy artillery fire, which poured canister and shell and solid shot into their ranks from the front and on both sides with frightful results. The ground was so thickly strewn with dead bodies as seriously to impede the movements of renewed attack. These repeated assaults in such good order caused some fear on the part of General Lee that they might eventually break his lines, and he conveyed his anxiety to General Longstreet, but his fears proved groundless.

General Cobb, who had so gallantly defended the Confederate position at the sunken road, against the onslaughts of the Federals, fell mortally wounded and was carried from the field.

His command was handed to Kershaw, who took his place in this desperate struggle. The onrushing Federals fell almost in battalions; the dead and wounded lay in heaps. Late in the day the dead bodies, which had become frozen from the extreme cold, were placed in front of the soldiers as a protection to shield the living.

The steadiness of the Union troops and the silent and determined heroism of the rank and file in these repeated but hopeless assaults upon the Confederate works were marvelous indeed, and will go down in history as a monument to the memory of those who were engaged in this terrible conflict.

After these disastrous attempts to carry the works of the Confederate left it was night; the Federals had retired; hope was abandoned, and it was seen that the day was lost for the Union forces. The shattered Army of the Potomac sought to gather and care for the wounded. The beautiful Fredericksburg of a few days before now had put on a different appearance. Ancestral homes were turned into hospitals. The charming drives and stately groves, and the pleasure grounds of the colonial days, were not filled with grand carriages and gay parties, but with war horses, soldiers and other military equipments, and had put on the gloom that follows in the wake of a defeated army after a great battle.

The plan of Burnside had ended in failure. In his report of the battle to Washington he gave reasons for the issue, and in a manly way took the responsibility upon himself and most highly commended his officers and men.

President Lincoln's verdict of this battle is reverse to the unanimous opinions of the historians. In his reply to Burnside's report of the battle he says, "Although you were not successful, the attempt was not an error, nor the failure other than accident."

After the battle the wounded lay on the field in their agony, exposed to the freezing cold for forty-eight hours before they were cared for. Many were burned by the long dead grass becoming ignited by the cannon fire.

The scene witnessed was dreadful and heart-rending. The Union loss was about 12,000, and the Confederates less than half that number. The Union army was withdrawn across the river under the cover of darkness, and the battle of Fredericksburg had passed into history.

Burnside, at his own request, was relieved of the command of the Army of the Potomac, which was handed to General Joseph Hooker.

THE BATTLE OF CHANCELLORSVILLE

After the battle of Fredericksburg the Union army went into winter quarters at Falmouth, only a few miles away, while the Confederates took up their encampment for the winter at Fredericksburg.

General Joseph Hooker, who was popularly known as "Fighting Joe Hooker," had succeeded General Burnside in command of the Army of the Potomac, which numbered about 130,000 men, while that of the Confederates numbered about 60,000.

Hooker conceived the idea to divide his army and leave Sedgwick with about 40,000 men to make a feint upon the Confederates, stationed about Fredericksburg, and himself with the remainder of the army to move around Lee's army and take a position at

Chancellorsville, a small place in a wilderness country only a few miles from Fredericksburg, and by doing this, take Lee by surprise. These plans of Hooker have been considered by war historians as being well laid if they had been carried out. Lee was on the alert, and had heard of Hooker's plans, and was not to be caught in the trap. Lee, paying little attention to Sedgwick, east of Fredericksburg, had turned to face Hooker. By rapid night marches he met Hooker's army before it reached its destination. His advance columns were pushed back by the Federals, who succeeded in taking the position which was assigned to them, Meade on the left and Slocum on the right, with adequate support in the rear. All was in readiness and had favorable positions when, to the amazement of all the officers, Hooker ordered the whole army to fall back to the position it had occupied the day before, thereby leaving the advantage with Lee, who moved his forces up to the positions which the Federals evacuated and began feeling the Federal lines with some cannonading during the evening of May 1st.

The Confederates were in extreme danger, having one large army in their front and another almost as large as theirs in their rear near Fredericksburg. But Lee decided to make one great and decisive blow at Hooker in front. During the night of May 1st Lee held council with "Stonewall" Jackson and accepted a plan laid out by him for Jackson to take part of the army and move around through the dense wood and rough country and fall upon the right flank of the enemy.

Early on the morning of May 2d the cannonading began its death-song and the infantry was brought into action. Before long Jackson began, with a portion of the army, to move off the field, and Hooker, observing this, believed that Lee's army was in full retreat on Richmond. This movement proved to be the undoing of Hooker's army, as Jackson was making for his right flank. It was about five o'clock in the afternoon when Jackson broke from the woods in a charge upon the unsuspecting troops of Hooker's right which was under Howard.

The approach of Jackson's forces was first intimated to the Federals by the bending of shrubbery, the stampede of rabbits and squirrels, and the flocks of birds in wild flight from the woods. First appeared a few skirmishers, then the rattling of musketry and the incessant roar of cannon. On the Confederates came in their impetuous charge. The charge was so unexpected and terrific that they carried everything before them. The Federal lines were swept as by tidal waves and rolled up like a scroll.

This crowning and final stroke of Jackson's military genius was the result of his own carefully worked-out plan, which had been approved by Lee.

General Hooker was spending the evening at his headquarters at the Chancellor House, rejoicing, as he thought, that Jackson was in full retreat and everything appeared to be going well. Presently the roar of battle became louder and louder on his right and an officer came up at full speed to notify him that his right was being fiercely attacked, was giving away, and would soon be in utter rout. Hooker made haste to the scene of battle and passed through brigade after brigade of his forces in retreat and confusion.

He was successful in having Berry re-form his division and charge the Confederates with fixed bayonets, which partly stopped the Confederates' advance. This gave the Federal artillery a few minutes to prepare itself for action. They finally succeeded in stopping the Confederate advance.

The mighty turmoil was silenced as darkness gathered. The two hostile forces were concealed in the darkness watching each other. Finally, at midnight, the order, "Forward!" was given in subdued tones to Sickle's corps. They stealthily advanced upon the Confederate position and at heavy loss gained the position sought for.

Between Hooker's and Sedgwick's divisions of the army stood the Confederate army flushed with the victory of the day, immediately in front of Sedgwick was Fredericksburg, beyond which loomed Marye's Heights, strongly guarded by Washington's artillery of the Confederates. These Heights were the battleground of a few months before when Burnside tried in vain to drive the Confederates from their crest.

Shortly after midnight Sedgwick began his march against Marye's Heights that was fraught with peril and death. At the foot of the slope were the stone wall and the sunken road, which was the battleground of a few months before in the battle of Fredericksburg. The crest and slopes bristled with Confederate cannon and musket. Sedgwick made his attack directly upon the stone wall in the face of a terrible storm of artillery and musketry. The first assault failed, but the second met with more success, as they succeeded in driving the Confederates from their strong position at the point of the bayonet by their overwhelming numbers. Sedgwick pushed on to attack Lee in the rear, but Lee was aware of his advance and dispatched General Early with a strong force to hold him in check and thus prevent his juncture with Hooker's army at Chancellorsville. Lee's army and that of Hooker's had been engaged since early morning in deadly combat.

While this engagement was at its height General Hooker, while leaning against a pillar on the porch of the Chancellor House, was stunned and felled to the ground and for some time it was thought that he was killed. This was done by a cannon ball, which shattered the pillar against which he was leaning. This injury incapacitated Hooker from active service the balance of the day and he gave orders for his army to retire, which was reluctantly done by his subordinate officers. When his columns began to retire from the field the Confederates increased their artillery fire, which played upon the retreating columns in blue. This fire marked the doom of the old Chancellor House, where Hooker had headquarters. The brick walls were pierced through by cannon balls and shells exploded in the upper rooms, setting the building on fire. Fragments of the demolished chimneys rained down upon the wounded in the lower rooms.

During the entire day's battle there were nineteen women and children, including some slaves, in the cellar where they had taken refuge. They were all removed before the complete destruction of the house by fire.

The long, deep trenches, full of Federal and Confederate dead, told the awful story of Chancellorsville. This scene will never be forgotten by the survivors of the battle. This was one of the greatest battles yet fought on the American Continent, and has gone down in history as being one of the greatest of modern times.

The Union loss was about 17,000, while that of the Confederates was about 13,000.

Late in the evening of the first day's battle General "Stonewall" Jackson was mortally wounded, in which the South suffered incalculable loss. After his brilliant flank march and the evening attack on Hooker's army had been driven home, at half-past eight, Jackson had ridden beyond his lines to reconnoiter for the final advance. By the sudden fire of musketry in his front, he discovered that he was within the enemy's lines. His party, suddenly turning back and riding at full speed, was mistook by his own men for the enemy, and his men, firing a volley of musketry, killed and wounded several of Jackson's party and mortally wounded Jackson by two shots in the left arm and one in his right hand. He was taken from his horse by the officers who were with him, among whom was A. P. Hill. It was found that there was no immediate conveyance for him to be carried within his lines. Presently the enemy discovered the commotion and mistaking it as an advance of the Confederate lines, began to shell the immediate vicinity with grape and canister, which necessitated the party with Jackson to lie down to escape the shower of lead which poured over them. The scene about them was an awful one. The air was pierced by the shrieks of shells and the cries of the wounded. Finally a stretcher was secured and Jackson was carried to the rear. One of the bearers was shot down and his place was taken by another. During the turmoil General W. D. Pender was met, who expressed the fear that his lines must fall back. General Jackson, in a clear voice, "You must hold your ground, General Pender; you must hold your ground to the last, sir." This was his last order to a subordinate officer.

It was first thought that Jackson's wounds would not prove fatal, but he developed pneumonia and gradually grew worse, and on the morning of May 10th it was apparent that he had only a few hours to live; at times he was unconscious and his mind apparently wandered on previous battlefields. During one of his unconscious moments he suddenly cried out, "Order A. P. Hill to prepare for action. Pass the infantry to the front!"

He then became silent and weak, and his last words were: "Let us cross over the river and rest in the shade of the trees."

When Lee heard that Jackson had fallen he said: "Any victory would be dear at such a price." It is thought by many that the result at Gettysburg would have been different had "The Great Flanker" lived to have been there. Henderson, the British war historian, said the fame of "Stonewall" Jackson is no longer the exclusive property of Virginia and the South; it has become the birthright of every man privileged to call himself an American.

THE SIEGE OF VICKSBURG

Vicksburg, often called "The Gibraltar of the West," is situated on the east bank of the Mississippi River, where the river makes a great bend and the east bank of the same makes up from the river in a bluff about 200 feet.

Here at Vicksburg about 100,000 men and a powerful fleet of many gunboats and ironclads for forty days and nights fought to decide whether the Confederate states should be cut in twain; whether the great river should flow free to the gulf.

The Confederate cannon, situated on the high bluff along the river front at Vicksburg, commanded the waterway for miles in either direction, while the obstacles in the way of a land approach were almost equally insurmountable.

The object of the Federal army was to gain control of the entire course of the river that it might, in the language of President Lincoln, "Roll unvexed to the sea," and to separate the Confederate states so as to hinder them from getting supplies and men for their armies from the southwest.

The great problem of the Federals was how to get control of Vicksburg. This great question was left to General Grant to work out.

In June, 1862, the Confederates, under General Van Dorn, numbering 15,000 men, occupied and fortified Vicksburg. Van Dorn was a man of great energy. In a short time he had hundreds of men at work planting batteries, digging rifle-pits, mounting heavy guns and building bomb-proof magazines. All through the summer the work progressed and by the coming of winter the city was a veritable Gibraltar.

In the last days of June the combined fleet, under Farragut and Porter, arrived below the Confederate stronghold. They had on board about 3,000 troops and a large supply of implements required in digging trenches. The engineers conceived the idea of cutting a new channel for the Mississippi through a neck of land on the Louisiana side opposite Vicksburg and thereby change the course of the river and leave Vicksburg high and dry.

While General Williams was engaged in the task of diverting the mighty river across the peninsula Farragut stormed the Confederate batteries with his fleet, but failed to silence Vicksburg's cannon guards. He then determined to dash past the fortifications with his fleet, trusting to the speed of his vessels and the stoutness of their armor to survive the tremendous cannonade that would fall upon them.

Early on the morning of June 28th his vessels moved forward and after several hours of terrific bombardment with the loss of three vessels, passed through the raging inferno to the waters above Vicksburg.

Williams and his men, including 1,000 negroes, labored hard to complete the canal, but a sudden rise in the river swept away the barriers with a terrific roar and many days of labor went for naught. This plan was at length abandoned and they all returned with the fleet during the last days of July to Baton Rouge, and Vicksburg was no more molested until the next spring.

In October General John C. Pemberton, a Philadelphian by birth, succeeded Van Dorn in command of the Confederate forces at Vicksburg. General Grant planned to divide the army of the Tennessee, Sherman taking part of it from Memphis down the Mississippi on transports while he would move overland with the rest of the army and coöperate with Sherman before Vicksburg. But the whole plan proved a failure, through the energies of Van Dorn and others of the Confederate army in destroying the Federal lines of communication.

Sherman, however, with an army of about 32,000 men, left Memphis on December 20th, and landed a few days later some miles above Vicksburg, and on the 29th made a daring attack on the Confederate lines at Chickasaw Bayou, and suffered a decisive repulse with a loss of 2,000 men.

Sherman now found the northern pathway to Vicksburg impassable and withdrew his men to the river, and, to make up triple disaster to the Federals, General Nathan Forest, one of the brilliant Confederate cavalry leaders, with 2,500 horsemen, dashed through the country west of Grant's army, tore up many miles of railroad and destroyed all telegraph lines and thus cut off all communication of the Federals.

In the meantime General Van Dorn pounced upon Holly Springs, capturing the guard of 1,500 men and burning Grant's great store of supplies, estimated to be worth a million and a half dollars, thus leaving Grant without supplies, and for many days without communication with the outside world. It was not until about the middle of January that he heard, through Washington, of the defeat of Sherman at Chickasaw Bayou.

Grant changed his plan of attack and decided to move his army below Vicksburg and approach the city from the south. Another plan was to cut a channel through the peninsula opposite Vicksburg and again try the project of changing the bed of the Mississippi so as to leave Vicksburg some miles inland. For six weeks thousands of men worked on this ditch; early in March the river began to rise and on the morning of the 8th it broke through the embankments and the men had to run for their lives. Many horses were drowned and great numbers of implements submerged. The "Father of waters" had put a decisive veto on the project, and the same was abandoned.

On the night of April 16th Porter ran past the batteries of Vicksburg with his fleet after days of preparation. They left their station near the mouth of the Yazoo about nine o'clock. Suddenly the flash of musketry fire pierced the darkness. A storm of shot and shell was rained upon the passing vessels. The water of the river was lashed into foam by the shot and shell from the batteries. The gunboats answered with their cannon. The air was filled with flying missiles. The transport, Henry Clay, caught fire and burned to the water's edge. By three in the morning the fleet was below the city and ready to coöperate with Grant's army.

Grant's army at that time numbered about 43,000 men, and he decided to make a campaign into the interior of Mississippi while waiting for General Banks from Baton Rouge to join him. The Confederate army under Pemberton numbered about 40,000, and about 15,000 more Confederates were at Jackson, Miss., under command of General Joseph E. Johnston. It was against Johnston's army that Grant decided to move. Johnston, on being attacked by Grant, fell back from Jackson and took a position on Champion's Hill, where a hard battle was fought in which the Confederates were greatly outnumbered and gave way in confusion. Part of Pemberton's army had arrived and was engaged in this battle. Pemberton retreated towards Vicksburg, closely followed by Grant, and several short engagements between the two armies took place on the road to Vicksburg. The Federal army now invested the city, occupying the surrounding hills. Around the doomed city gleamed the thousands of bayonets of the Union army. The city was filled with soldiers and the citizens of the country who had fled there for refuge and were now penned in.

On May 22d Grant ordered a grand assault by his whole army. The troops, flushed with their victories of the last few days, were eager for the attack. It is said that his columns were made up with his taller soldiers in front and the second in stature in the next line, and so on down, so as to save exposure to the fire of the enemy.

At the appointed time the order was passed down the line to move forward, and the columns leaped from their hiding places and started on their disastrous march in the face of a murderous fire from the defenders of the city, only to be mowed down by the sweeping fire from the Confederate batteries. Others came, crawling over the bodies of their fallen comrades, but at every charge they were met by the missiles of death. Thus it continued hour after hour until the coming of darkness. The assault had failed and the Union forces retired within their entrenchments before the city. This is considered as one of the most brave and disastrous assaults of the war.

The army now settled down to the wearisome siege, and for six weeks they encircled the city with trenches, approaching nearer and nearer to the defending walls. One by one the defending batteries were silenced. On the afternoon of June 25th a redoubt of the Confederate works was blown up with a mine. When the same exploded the Federals began to dash into the opening, only to meet with a withering fire from an interior parapet which the Confederates had constructed in the anticipation of this event.

Grant was constantly receiving reënforcements, and before the end of the siege his army numbered 70,000.

Day and night the roar of artillery continued without ceasing. Shrieking shells from Porter's fleet rose in grand curves, either bursting in midair or on the streets of the city, spreading havoc in all directions.

The people of the city burrowed into the ground for safety, their walls of clay being shaken by the roaring battles that raged above the ground. The supply of food became scarcer day by day, and by the end of June the entire city was in a complete famine. They had been living for several days upon corn meal, beans and mule meat, and were now facing their last enemy, death by starvation.

At ten o'clock on the morning of July 3d the firing ceased and a strange quietness rested over all. Pemberton had opened negotiations with Grant for the capitulation of the city. It is strange to say that on this very day the final chapter at Gettysburg was being written.

On the following morning Pemberton marched his 30,000 men out of the city and surrendered them as prisoners of war. They were released on parole.

This was the largest army ever surrendered at one time.

BATTLE OF GETTYSBURG

Our colonial fathers from North and South fought together when they brought this republic into being, defended it together in the war of 1812, and triumphed together when they carried the Stars and Stripes into the heritage of the Montezumas. The final and crucial test of the republic's strength and durability was the combat on the field of battle in the war between the states. The battle of Gettysburg is conceded to be the turning point in that war. Abraham Lincoln said in his Gettysburg address, in November, 1863: "This nation, conceived in liberty and dedicated to the proposition that all men are created equal, is now engaged in a great civil war, testing whether this nation, or any nation so conceived and so dedicated, can long endure."

The great question of that day was the question of state rights and relationship between state and federal government.

It had now come to the point where it could not be determined in the councils of peace, although the illustrious Henry Clay and other statesmen of his day had been the means of successfully deferring from time to time this crisis for almost a half century.

Gettysburg is a small, quiet town among the hills of Adams county, in southeastern Pennsylvania, and in 1863 contained about 1,500 inhabitants. It had been founded by James Gettys in about 1780. He probably never dreamed that his name, thus given to the village, would become famous in history for all time.

The hills around Gettysburg are little more than general swells of ground, and many of them were covered with timber when the legions of the North and South fought out the destinies of the republic on those memorable July days in 1863.

Lee's army was flushed with the victories of Fredericksburg and Chancellorsville, and public opinion was demanding an invasion of the North.

Lee crossed the Potomac early in June, after leaving General Stuart with his cavalry and a part of Hill's corps to prevent Hooker from pursuing. He began to concentrate his army around Hagerstown, Md., and prepare for a campaign in Pennsylvania. His army was organized into three corps under the respective commands of Longstreet, Ewell and A. P. Hill. Lee had driven his army so as to enter Pennsylvania by different routes, and to assess the towns along the way with large sums of money. In the latter part of June Lee was startled by the information that Stuart had failed to detain Hooker, and that the Federals were in hot pursuit. He soon conceived that the two armies must soon come together in a mighty death struggle, which meant that a great battle must be fought, a greater battle than this western world has heretofore known, which is claimed by historians as being one of the decisive battles of the world.

The Army of the Potomac had changed leaders, and George Gordon Meade was now its commander, having succeeded Hooker on June 28th. Thus for the third time the Army of the Potomac in ten months had a new commander.

The two great armies were scattered over portions of Maryland and southern Pennsylvania. Both were marching northward along parallel lines, the Federals endeavoring to stay between Lee's army and Washington. It was plain that they must soon come together in a gigantic conflict; but just where the shock of battle was to take place was yet unknown.

Meade sent General Buford in advance with 4,000 cavalry to intercept the Confederate advance guard.

On the night of June 30th Buford encamped on a hill a mile west from Gettysburg, and here on the following morning the great battle had its beginning.

On the morning of July 1st the two armies were still well scattered, the extremes forty miles apart. General Reynolds, with two corps of the Union army was but a few miles away and was hastening to Gettysburg, while Longstreet and Hill were approaching from the west, with Hill's corps several miles in advance.

Buford opened battle against the advance division of Hill's corps under General Heth. Reynolds soon joined and the first day's battle was now in full progress. General Reynolds, while placing his troops in line of battle early in the day, received a death shot in the head by a Confederate sharpshooter. This was a great loss to the Federals, as he was one of the bravest and most able generals in the Union army. No casualty of the war brought more widespread mourning to the North than the death of General John F. Reynolds. But even this calamity did not stay the fury of the battle.

Early in the afternoon the Federals were heavily reënforced, and A. P. Hill had arrived on the field with the balance of his corps, and the roar of battle was unceasing. About the middle of the afternoon a breeze lifted the smoke from the field and revealed that the Federals were falling back towards Gettysburg. They were hard pressed by the Confederates and were pushed back through the town with the loss of many prisoners. The Federals took a position on Cemetery Hill and the first day's battle was over.

If the Confederates had known the disorganized condition of the Federal troops, they might have pursued and captured a large part of the army.

It is thought by many that if "Stonewall" Jackson had lived to be there that at this particular time is where he would have delivered his crushing blow to the Federals and no doubt would have changed the final result of the battle. Meade was still some miles from the field, but on hearing of the death of Reynolds sent General Hancock to take command until he himself should arrive.

The Union loss on the first day was severe. A great commander had fallen and they had suffered the fearful loss of 10,000 men.

Hancock arrived late in the afternoon, after riding at full speed. His presence brought an air of confidence, and his promise of heavy reënforcements all tended to inspire renewed hope in the ranks of the discouraged army.

Meade reached the scene late at night and chose to make this field the place of a general engagement. Lee had come to the same decision, and both called on their outlying legions to make all possible speed to Gettysburg. The night was spent in the marshaling of troops, getting position, planting artillery, and bands playing at intervals on the arrival of new divisions on the field.

General Gordon says that during the night the sound of axes and the falling of trees in the Federal entrenchments could plainly be heard, and that he became convinced during the night that by morning they would be so well fortified on Cemetery Hill that their position would be almost impregnable, and that he succeeded in getting a council of officers during the night to take under advisement a night attack on the enemy, but was told that General Lee had given orders that no further attack should be made until Longstreet arrived, and he had not yet arrived.

The dawn of July 2d broke into a beautiful summer day. Both armies hesitated to begin the battle and remained inactive until in the afternoon.

The fighting on that day was confined chiefly to the two extremes, leaving the center inactive. Longstreet commanded the Confederate right and the Union left was commanded by General Daniel E. Sickles, whose division lay directly opposite that of Longstreet. The Confederate left was commanded by General Richard Ewell, who succeeded to the command of this division after the death of "Stonewall" Jackson at Chancellorsville. While the Federal right, stationed on Culp's Hill was commanded by General Slocum.

Between these armies was a hollow into which the anxious farmers had driven and penned large numbers of cattle, which they thought would be a place of safety, and could not conceive that any battle could affect this place of refuge, but when the battle began and the stream of shells was directed against Round Top this place of refuge became a raging inferno of bursting shells.

There was a gate at the entrance of the local cemetery at Gettysburg that had written on it this sign: "All persons found using firearms in these grounds will be prosecuted with the utmost rigor of the law." Many a soldier must have smiled at these words, for this gateway became the very center of the crudest use of firearms yet seen on this "terrestrial ball."

The plan of General Meade was to have General Sickles connect his division with that of Hancock and extend southward near the base of the Round Tops. Sickles found this ground, in his opinion, low and disadvantageous and advanced his division to higher ground in front, placing his men along the Emmettsburg road and back toward the

Trostle farm and the wheat-field, thus forming an angle at the peach orchard, thus leaving this division alone in its position far in advance of the other Federal lines. This position taken by Sickles was in disobedience of orders from General Meade, and was considered by Meade, as well as President Lincoln, as being a great mistake, but General Sickles always maintained that he did right, and that his position was well taken.

Longstreet was quick to see this apparent mistake and marched his troops along Sickles' front entirely overlapping the left wing of the Union army. Lee gave orders to Longstreet to make a general attack, and the boom of his cannon announced the beginning of the second day's battle. The Union forces answered quickly with their batteries and the fight extended from the peach orchard along the whole line to the base of Little Round Top. The musketry opened all along the line until there was one continuous roar. Longstreet swept forward in a line or battle a mile and a half long. He pressed back the Union forces and for a time it looked as though the Federals would be routed in utter confusion.

At the extreme left, near the Trostle house, was stationed John Biglow, in command of a Massachusetts battery, with orders to hold his position at all hazards. He defended his position well, but was finally routed with great loss by overwhelming numbers. This attack was made by Longstreet again and again, and was one of the bloodiest spots on the field at Gettysburg.

The most desperate struggle of the day was to get possession of Little Round Top, which was the key to the whole battleground west and south of Cemetery Ridge. General Longstreet sent General Hood with his division to occupy it. The Federals, under General Warren, defended this position and were charged on by General Hood's division with fixed bayonets time after time, which finally became a hand-to-hand conflict, but the Confederates were pressed down the hillside at the point of the bayonet, and thus was ended one of the most severe hand-to-hand conflicts yet known.

Little Round Top was saved to the Union army, but the cost was appalling. The hill was covered with hundreds of the slain. Many of the Confederate sharpshooters had taken position among the crevasses of the rocks in the Devil's Den, where they could overlook the position on Little Round Top, and their unerring aim spread death among the Federal officers. General Weed was mortally wounded, and, as General Hazlett was stooping to receive his last message, a sharpshooter's bullet laid him dead across the body of his chief.

During this attack, and for some time thereafter, the battle continued in the valley below, where many thousands were engaged. Longstreet and Sickles were engaged in a determined conflict, and it was apparent to all engaged that a decisive battle was being fought, and they were making a determined effort. Sickles' line was being pressed back to the base of the hill. His leg was shattered by a bursting shell, while scores of his officers and thousands of his men lay on the field to dream of battlefields no more. The coming of darkness ended the struggle. This valley has been rightly called the "Valley of Death."

While this battle was going on in this part of the field another was being fought at the other extreme end of the lines. General Ewell was making an attack on Cemetery Hill and Culp's Hill, held by Slocum, who had been weakened by the sending of a large portion of his corps to the assistance of General Sickles. Ewell had three divisions, two of which were commanded by Generals Early and Johnston. Early made the attack on Cemetery Hill, but was repulsed after a bloody and desperate hand-to-hand fight. Johnston's attack on Culp's Hill was more successful, but was at length repulsed after the Federals had been heavily reënforced.

Thus closed the second day's battle of Gettysburg. The harvest of death had been great. The Federal loss during the two days was about 20,000 men; the Confederate loss was nearly as great. The Confederates had gained an apparent advantage on Culp's Hill, but the Union lines, except as to this point, were unbroken.

On the night of July 2d Lee held council of war with his generals and decided to make a grand assault on Meade's center the following day. Against this decision Longstreet protested in vain, but Lee was encouraged by the arrival of Pickett's division and Stuart's cavalry, which had not yet been engaged. Meade had held council with his officers, and had come to a like decision to defend.

That night a brilliant July moon shed its luster upon the ghastly field, over which thousands of men lay unable to rise. With many their last battle was over, but there were great numbers of wounded who were calling for the kindly touch of a helping hand. Nor did they call wholly in vain. They were carried to the improvised hospitals where they were given attention. The dead were buried in unknown graves soon to be forgotten except by their loving mothers.

All through the night the Confederates were massing their artillery along Seminary Ridge. The disabled horses were being replaced by others. The ammunition was being replenished, and all was being made ready for their work of destruction on the morrow.

The Federals were diligently laboring in the moonlight arranging their batteries on Cemetery Hill. The coming of morning revealed the two parallel lines of cannon which signified too well the story of what the day would bring forth.

On the first day of July, 1863, Pickett's division was encamped near Chambersburg, Penn., about twenty miles from Gettysburg.

This division was composed of three brigades, commanded by Armistead, Garnett and Kemper. They had no intimation that they would be called on to take part in the battle that was going on at Gettysburg. They had been following up as the rear guard of the Army of Northern Virginia.

BATTLE OF ANTIETAM

The men were quietly sleeping after a most fatiguing march, and many no doubt dreaming of their homes along the Atlantic and Chesapeake, and others of their beautiful mountains and beautiful valleys, and in their dreams, perhaps, felt the warm kiss of their loved ones. All at once the long roll was sounded, and these visions vanished as they awoke and realized that grim war was still rampant. The division was ordered, about 1 A. M. on the morning of July 2d, to pack up and make ready to march, and while doing this it was rumored along the lines that Hood's division of Texans had been repulsed in charging Cemetery Heights at Gettysburg with frightful loss, and that it was the intention of General Lee that their division should charge the strong position as a forlorn hope.

About 3 A. M., on July 2d, the division began to move towards Gettysburg and marched as rapidly as circumstances would permit, as the roads were blocked with wagons, artillery, and the wounded of both armies. At length it arrived at about two o'clock in the evening within two miles of Gettysburg and immediately went into camp. While they were doing so a courier rode up and informed the officers that McLaws' division of Georgians had just made a charge on Cemetery Heights and had been repulsed with great slaughter. This division, together with Hood's and Pickett's, made up Longstreet's corps, and it seemed that each of his divisions was to have the honor of making an assault on Cemetery Heights. General Pickett now informed his men that he had orders to hurl his division against this position on the next day unless the artillery should succeed in dislodging the enemy.

On the following day this division took position in line of battle directly behind the Confederate artillery line on Seminary Ridge, with a line of timber between, and had orders to lie down. General Lee had massed in front of the division about 120 pieces of artillery, and they were to open on Cemetery Heights and endeavor if possible to dislodge the enemy. This cannonading began about noon, and was answered by the enemy with a hundred pieces. A more terrific fire has never been witnessed by man than occurred there on that July afternoon. The earth was shaken by its roar, such as probably the younger Pliny mentioned in his description of the eruption of Vesuvius when Pompeii and Herculaneum were destroyed. The sky was black with smoke, and livid with the flame belching from the mouth of the cannon.

During all this cannonading Pickett's division was lying awaiting it to cease. Round shot whistled through the trees, shells burst over their heads, dealing destruction within their ranks. The shot and shell from their enemy's guns that passed over the artillery invariably fell in the ranks of Pickett's division, which seemed doomed to destruction without even the opportunity of firing a gun. While this cannonading was going on, General Armistead and the other brigade commanders passed along in front of their respective commands informing their men that unless the artillery succeeded in dislodging the enemy from Cemetery Heights, they were to charge this position. Although this had been tried by the respective divisions of McLaw and Hood, and in each instance had been repulsed with great slaughter, yet they seemed determined to win for Virginia and the Confederate states a name which would be handed down to posterity in honor, and which would be spoken of in pride by not only Virginia but by all America. In this particular they succeeded, for not only have their foes accorded them a crown of laurels, but England spoke words of praise for these men, whose Anglo-Saxon blood nerved them to such a deed.

All at once the terrible cannonading ceased, and the stillness of death prevailed. General Pickett rode along the line informing his men that the artillery had not succeeded in driving the enemy from their strong position. Word was passed down the line from the right that they were to charge. All were on their feet in a moment and ready; not a sound was heard; not a shot was fired from any part of the field. The command, "Forward!" was given, and in five minutes they had passed through the strip of woods that lay between them and the artillery, and as they emerged from the cover and passed through the artillery line the artillerymen raised their hats and cheered them on their way. They also passed through Lane's brigade of Wilcox's division, whose men were waiting for orders to support the charge. General Garnett was leading the center, General Kemper on the right, and General Armistead was leading the left of the division with a swarm of skirmishers in front. The smoke had cleared away and revealed the long line of the Federal position on Cemetery Heights, which was about a mile distant.

When the Federals observed the advance of Pickett's division, which they had anticipated, they opened fire, which at first ranged over the advancing columns, but before they had marched half the distance they began to get range on them. The Confederate lines advanced steadily and in full confidence. A band on the extreme right continued to play "Dixie," "The Girl I Left Behind Me," and other familiar airs of the day. The division was marching directly towards Hancock's position, this objective point having been given Pickett by General Lee, but after passing through Wilcox's division in waiting Pickett caused each of his three brigades to make a half-wheel to the left. This, being well executed, was attended with some loss of time.

The Federal artillery soon began its death work of destruction. Pickett's division had been quite near this grim monster before, but on this occasion he seemed to be pressing on them steadily and closely, which was enough to make the bravest quail under his ghastly appearance. The Federals seem to have exhausted their ammunition in some places in the artillery lines. This being discovered by Pickett, gave him courage, and he caused his division to move up quickly. Crossing several fields inclosed by strong fences, he at length reached the base of the elevation. He once more changed his direction by a half-wheel to the right, halting to rectify his lines. His division pushed on, but great gaps were being cut in his lines by the grape and canister from the Federal artillery, causing such wide openings that the division had to be halted and dressed first to the right and then to the left, obliquing and filling up the lines. They were now in close range of the Federal lines and were being fired upon from behind a stone wall, and their ranks were fast melting away.

"Death was upon every breeze,
And lurked in every flower."

The division pressed on. Round shot, shell, canister and rifle balls were poured into them at close range from the front, and a battery on Round Top raked the line from the right.

Pickett was expecting to be supported by Pettigrew's brigade on the left, and Lane's brigade on the right. Those brigades, however, were coming up, but were being met by such strong opposition that they were entirely outdistanced and fell back finally with Pickett's retreat, thus leaving Pickett with his three brigades alone in front. The Confederate ranks were thinning as far as eye could see. Garnett was killed leading his brigade, his being in the lead. Kemper, coming up next to the distance of sixty yards behind, brought his brigade to a halt to give Armistead time to come up for the last and final charge.

They were fired upon by the enemy, posted along the edge of the woods. This murderous fire almost disorganized them. Armistead, urging his men forward with his hat on his sword, holding it up as a guide, crossed over the Union breastworks, and for a time the Confederates seemed to gain some advantage, but were presently surrounded by overwhelming numbers. General Armistead was mortally wounded, and nearly all the other officers of the division were either killed or wounded.

Pickett, seeing the hopelessness of the charge, ordered a retreat of his shattered lines.

Out of 4,800 men that followed Pickett, scarcely 1,200 to 1,300 got back into the Confederate lines. Out of eighteen field officers and four generals, Pickett and one lieutenant colonel alone remained unharmed.

Pickett's division, together with the supporting brigades under Lane and Pettigrew, numbered about 14,000 men. Where General Armistead fell is considered to be the highest point, figuratively speaking, that was reached by the Southern Confederacy.

Pickett's charge will be remembered by all future Americans as the English remember that of the Light Brigade, and the French that of the old guard under Marshal Ney at Waterloo.

The battle of Gettysburg was now over. The loss was about 50,000 men, which was about equally divided between the two armies.

General Lee decided to lead his army back to Virginia. The Confederates were much discouraged, for on this same day Vicksburg had been surrendered to General Grant.

All through the night of July 3d Lee's army was making ready to march and at the break of day A. P. Hill swung his corps into line of march through a downpour of rain. The next to follow was Longstreet's corps, which followed close upon A. P. Hill, and the last to leave was Ewell's corps, and the retreat was covered by Stuart's cavalry.

General Hood had with him 4,000 prisoners. The wounded were carried with the retreat in wagons and other ways of conveyance, and were under the charge of General Imboden.

BATTLE OF CHICKAMAUGA

This battle derives its name from Chickamauga Creek, which is but a few miles from Chattanooga, Tenn., and is considered one of the greatest battles of modern times. It was exceeded in our Civil war only by Gettysburg and the Wilderness; compares with Waterloo, and twice bloodier than Wagram or Austerlitz. General D. H. Hill said that he had never seen the Federal dead lie so thickly on the ground save in front of the sunken wall at Fredericksburg. The late General John B. Gordon, whose pen was never weary of writing the praises of the Confederate soldiers, said that in his opinion the battle of Chickamauga was even greater than that of Gettysburg, but it is thought that he was somewhat partial to Chickamauga, having been reared there, and when a boy fished in Chickamauga Creek, and had ridden behind his father over the country which was later made a great battlefield.

General Braxton Bragg was in command of the Confederate army, known as the Army of the Tennessee, which was concentrated around Chattanooga.

General Rosecrans was in command of the Federal army, known as the Army of the Cumberland. It was made up of three corps under

Generals Crittenden, Thomas and McCook. They began to advance on Chattanooga and endanger Bragg's line of communication.

On September 8th Bragg abandoned Chattanooga and fell back toward Rome, Ga. The Federals took possession of the city of Chattanooga. Rosecrans, believing that Bragg was in full retreat, ordered Crittenden to pursue. Meanwhile Bragg was concentrating his forces near Lafayette, about twenty-five miles from Chattanooga. He was joined by Generals S. B. Buckner and Breckinridge. General Longstreet was hastening from Virginia with about 12,000 men from Lee's army to join him, the men being fresh from the field of Gettysburg.

Rosecrans' army was somewhat divided, as he was not expecting a general battle. Bragg was quick to grasp this opportunity of making a general assault on the Union forces while they were divided. The attack was made on the 13th of September by General Polk, but from some misapprehension of orders he did not move in time, and thus gave Rosecrans time to unite his forces, thus losing Bragg this opportunity of breaking up the Army of the Cumberland.

The Federal forces under Crittenden now took position at Gordon's Mills, on the left bank of Chickamauga Creek, and the remainder of their troops were within supporting distance, and were under the command of Thomas and McCook, the total Union strength being estimated at about 60,000 men.

The Confederate army lay on the east side of the stream, and was under the immediate command of Generals Polk, D. H. Hill and Buckner.

On the 18th Longstreet arrived with his troops. Thus the two mighty armies were now face to face.

Bragg endeavored to flank the Federal left and thus intervene between it and Chattanooga, and on the morning of September 19th the Confederates, under General Polk, made a grand assault upon the Federal left, under General Thomas. Meanwhile the Federal right was being heavily pressed by General Hood, commanding Longstreet's corps. This was kept up the entire day and when darkness came the

Federals had been forced back from the creek, but the result was indecisive.

During the night preparations were made for the renewal of the battle on the next morning, which was Sunday, September 20th.

It is strange to say that some of the greatest battles of the war were fought on Sunday.

General Longstreet now took command of his troops which had arrived, but part of his corps did not arrive in time for the battle, having been delayed on trains that were behind time. This brought their strength up to equal that of the Federals.

General Thomas had taken position on Snodgrass Hill, and was anticipating a Confederate attack, which was made late in the morning by General Polk, who was supported by Generals Breckinridge and Patrick Cleburne, the last-named being an Irishman formerly from the County of Cork.

This assault was made time after time with desperate loss to both sides. At length, by some misunderstanding of orders, one of the Federal divisions under General Wood withdrew from its position. By this movement a large opening was made in the center of their battle line.

This was quickly taken advantage of by three divisions of the Confederates, which rushed in with an impetus that was irresistible.

General Hood, one of the Confederate division commanders, was severely wounded in this movement with a minie ball, and was carried from the field.

The Federals under Wood, Sheridan and Van Cleve were driven from the field. General Longstreet now assumed chief command, and here gave a fine exhibition of his military genius. He succeeded in separating the two wings of the opposing army. The right wing already being in full retreat, he wheeled and compelled the further withdrawal of Federal troops in order to save being surrounded. The retreating Federals fled in confusion toward Chattanooga, after suffering the loss of several thousand prisoners and forty pieces of artillery.

The Confederates now concentrated their attack upon Thomas, who had taken position on a ridge. They were led by the indomitable Longstreet, but were repulsed and hurled back with fearful slaughter. The Confederates were endeavoring to flank Thomas' division by sending Hinzman to the left and Kershaw with his divisions to get in the rear. The fighting grew fiercer and at intervals was hand-to-hand, and continued the entire afternoon.

This attack on Thomas is considered one of the heaviest made on a single point during the war. General Thomas, in his stand at Chickamauga, won for himself the name "The Rock of Chickamauga." He was one of the bravest and most able generals in the Union army, being a Virginian by birth.

Under the cover of darkness Thomas withdrew his army in good order to Rossville, and the following day joined Rosecrans in Chattanooga.

This battle is generally considered a Confederate victory, but left the Federal army in possession of Chattanooga. The personal daring and courage displayed in the ranks of both armies has never been excelled on any battlefield.

The total loss exceeded 30,000 men, which was probably divided about equal.

THE BATTLE OF LOOKOUT MOUNTAIN AND MISSIONARY RIDGE

After the battle of Chickamauga, Rosecrans' army was cooped up in Chattanooga, and his sources of supplies were entirely cut off by Bragg, except from the north of Chattanooga, by which he received his supplies over mountainous wagon roads, and, on account of heavy rains which fell during October, the roads became almost impassable. These trains were attacked by Confederate cavalry under General Forest, and in one day 300 wagons were destroyed and about 1,800 mules were either killed or captured. One soldier said "the mud was so deep that we could not travel by the road, but we got along pretty well by stepping from mule to mule as they lay dead by the way." Starvation threatened the camp, and the army must be relieved.

Vigorous measures were now taken. General Grant was now made commander of the western armies. He had about 80,000 men in addition to Burnside's force at Knoxville. The Confederates had about 60,000. General Sherman was directed to reënforce Grant at Chattanooga from Vicksburg and transported his forces by boat to Memphis, and from there marched overland.

The authorities at Washington also determined to reënforce Rosecrans from the Army of the Potomac, and 23,000 men, under General Hooker, were transported by rail to Chattanooga. This brought the Army of the Cumberland to numbers far exceeding those of the Confederates. The immediate command of all the Federal forces was given to General Thomas until such time as General Grant should arrive. Grant telegraphed to Thomas to hold Chattanooga at all hazards. Thomas replied, "I will do so till we starve."

The first and great question of the Federals was to relieve their line of supplies. General Hooker was sent with a portion of his troops against a strong position taken by some Confederates in Lookout Valley, and, after a short but decisive battle succeeded in driving the Confederates back, which left him in possession of the immediate country, and thus opened up a route to Brown's Ferry, over which a route for abundant supplies was at once available. This relieved the Army of the Cumberland of its perilous position.

Thomas was being reënforced from all sides; Hooker was already on the ground; Sherman was advancing rapidly from Memphis, while Burnside's forces at Knoxville offered protection for the left flank of the Federal army.

General Bragg had his forces in a line extending a distance of twelve miles across to Missionary Ridge, and was strengthened by entrenchments throughout the lowlands. He determined to attack Burnside at Knoxville, and dispatched Longstreet over his protest with 20,000 men to do this, thus weakening his extended lines. This has been considered a very great mistake of Bragg, as his total force was much less than had opposed Rosecrans at Chickamauga. Grant had now arrived and had assumed command of the entire Federal forces, and had planned to attack Bragg on November 24th, but on receiving information, which proved to be unreliable, that Bragg was preparing to retreat, he decided to make the attack on the 23d, and ordered Thomas to advance upon Bragg's center. This attack took the Confederates by surprise. After some severe fighting, they fell back more than a mile and left the Federals in command of some advantageous positions, thus ending the first day's battle.

Preparations were made during the night for a general engagement the next day.

Sherman was in command of the left wing, while Thomas held the center, and Hooker the right, and they had planned to sever communications between Bragg and Longstreet, and thus keep the Confederate army divided.

Early on the 24th Sherman moved against the Confederate right, and with little opposition occupied the northern end of Missionary Ridge. The Confederates, after discovering this advantageous position taken by Sherman, fought desperately in the afternoon to regain it, but were finally repulsed.

While this was going on, General Hooker, with a division of Sherman's army, was making a desperate struggle for the capture of Lookout Mountain, whose rugged crests towered above the clouds. This mountain was ably defended by the Confederates, but they were finally pushed back by overwhelming numbers and made their final stand within the breastworks about the Craven house, but were finally dislodged from this place and retired within their entrenchments in the valley.

This has been termed "The Battle in the Clouds."

BATTLE OF GETTYSBURG

On the morning of the 25th preparations were made for the final battle on Missionary Ridge. The attack was made by General Sherman, and it seemed that the Confederates must recede from the terrific onslaught, but they succeeded, after a stubborn struggle, in repulsing the Federals at this particular time, and they were pushed back by General Hardy, who captured several hundred prisoners. The Federals, quickly re-forming their lines, renewed the assault and, after waiting for Hooker to bring up his division, Grant ordered a general advance, and the battle was now on in earnest. Bragg opened on them from the crest of Missionary Ridge with fifty pieces of artillery and a line of musketry. Even this did not stop the impetuous charge. The first line of entrenchments of the Confederates was carried with little opposition, and, as the Confederates retired through other brigades, the confusion was great, and the retreat became almost a rout.

Had it not been for a division of North Carolinan soldiers under Major Weaver, who succeeded in rallying his troops, and was successful in holding the Federals in check, the retreat would have become a rout of the entire Confederate army.

This gave the Confederates a little time to rally their lines, and they were able to retire from the field in good order.

The battle was now over, and the field was left in possession of the Federals, Bragg retiring with his army into Georgia.

BATTLE OF THE WILDERNESS

This was one of the great battles of modern times, being second only to Gettysburg in our Civil war. Napoleon never fought a battle on the Continent of Europe that was equal to the Wilderness. It was three times bloodier than Austerlitz, after which battle it is said Napoleon's triumphant march from Freize to Paris was more grand than Queen Elizabeth's tour of England after the defeat of the Spanish Armada.

The Battle of the Wilderness, together with Spottsylvania, is thought to be more destructive to the Federal forces than both Antietam and Gettysburg combined.

On Lee's sudden departure from Gettysburg there were many stragglers left behind, who were taken prisoners by the Federals. Some of them were not aware that the army had gone; others, on account of slight wounds and sickness, were not able to keep up with the army.

Lee succeeded in crossing the Potomac above Harper's Ferry about the middle of July with but little opposition from the Federals, and led his army across the Rapidan, and there entrenched himself to dispute the Federals under General Meade, who had by this time succeeded in crossing the Potomac and was moving upon Culpeper Court House, at which place he concentrated his forces. There was but little fighting done during the remainder of the year, except an unsuccessful cavalry expedition under Kilpatrick, who sought to take Richmond by surprise.

During the early months of 1864 the authorities at Washington became discouraged with General Meade's management of the Army of the Potomac. They thought that he should have destroyed Lee's army on its retreat from Gettysburg; while it is now conceded that Meade's management was good, and that he did all that any general could have done under the circumstances. General Grant had come into great favor in the North on account of his successive victories in the West, and it was decided to give Grant command of all the Federal forces, with the rank of lieutenant-general. This high grade in command had been held only by Generals Washington and Scott, thus bringing together two great generals. One the idol of the North: the other of the South. Cæsar said he would rather be first man in a village in Gaul than second in Rome.

Grant found under his command in the Army of the Potomac 140,000 men.

Lee found under his command scarcely 60,000 men, but that spirit burned in the breast of his soldiers notwithstanding their defeat at Gettysburg and their loss of Vicksburg, that many hard battles would be fought before the heel of the invader should tread upon the streets of their cherished capital, Richmond.

Grant determined to move upon Richmond and by doing so began with the Wilderness a series of battles which are unequaled in history.

Grant's army was divided into three corps, commanded by Hancock, Warren and Sedgwick. Sheridan was in command of the cavalry. Burnside was in command of another division of the army, protecting the Orange and Alexandria railroad.

Lee's army consisted of three corps of infantry, commanded by Longstreet, Ewell and A. P. Hill, and the cavalry by Stuart. A notable fact in the organization of the Confederate army was the few changes made in commanders.

Early on the morning of May 4th Grant's army began crossing the Rapidan below Lee's entrenchments. This being anticipated by Lee, he at once prepared to set his own army in motion and throw himself across the path of his foe. Both armies were now near Chancellorsville, in a wilderness country, where a great battle had been fought the year before. This country was covered by underbrush and ragged foliage, with scrub pine, and dotted here and there with small clearings. This wilderness country was pierced by a few roads leading from the fords of the river. The Federals had advanced up these roads as far as the Wilderness Tavern, in which General Grant established his headquarters.

This wilderness country was entered by two roads from the southwest known as the "Old Orange Turnpike" and the "Orange Plank Road." Along these two roads the Confederates moved their army to meet the advancing hosts of the Federals, General Ewell leading his corps along the turnpike and A. P. Hill along the plank road. General Longstreet was hastening up from Gordonsville, and it was very evident that a great battle was near at hand.

On the morning of May 5th Ewell came in contact with Warren's corps at a cross-road near Parker's store, and this meeting precipitated the beginning of the great battle.

About this time it became known to General Grant that A. P. Hill was advancing by the plank road, and he ordered Sedgwick to entrench and prepare to receive the attack from A. P. Hill. Hill came up very soon, and the battle began in earnest. The musketry fire was continued with great severity until late in the evening without a decided advantage to either side. The loss was great and the Federals had suffered the loss of General Hays, who had been shot through the head. The Confederates had suffered the loss of General John M. Jones.

This ended the first day's struggle, and during the night both armies entrenched themselves directly in each other's front.

Early on the morning of May 6th the Federals were reënforced by Burnside's corps, and A. P. Hill by that of Longstreet.

General Grant issued orders for a general attack all along the line, and soon the battle was raging along the five-mile front, which became a hand-to-hand contest. Artillery played but little force in this battle, on account of the dense growth of timber and underbrush, and it was chiefly a battle of musketry.

The branches were cut from the trees by the leaden missiles, and saplings were mowed down as grass by a scythe.

The Confederates were finally driven back and seemed on the verge of a panic. At this moment General Lee rode through the lines to the front and called on his soldiers to follow him. This instantly gave courage to his army, which rallied and began to push the Federals back. General Lee was called back by his own men: "General Lee to the rear! General Lee to the rear!" This brave act on the part of General Lee, and the arrival of Longstreet, restored order and courage in the ranks, and they soon regained their lost position.

General Longstreet, while riding with Generals Kershaw and Jenkins, at the head of Jenkins' brigade, were mistaken for the enemy by their own men and fired on, and when the smoke lifted Longstreet and Jenkins were down—Longstreet seriously wounded, and Jenkins killed outright. This was a serious loss to the Confederacy, as they had suffered the loss of one general and had incapacitated another from service. A similar thing had occurred a year before at Chancellorsville when General Jackson was mortally wounded.

The fighting continued the rest of the day, the advantage being first with one side and then the other.

Darkness ended the two days' undecisive Battle of the Wilderness, one of the greatest struggles in history.

It was Grant's first measure of arms with General Lee. While Grant had been defeated in his plan to pass around Lee to Richmond, yet he had made a new record for the Army of the Potomac.

The loss of the Federals in killed and wounded was about 17,000, while that of the Confederates was about 12,000.

THE BATTLE OF SPOTTSYLVANIA COURT HOUSE

General John B. Gordon said that Spottsylvania furnished the longest roll of incessant musketry; the most splendid exhibition of heroism and personal daring by large numbers who, standing in the freshly spilled blood of their comrades, faced for so long a period and at so short a range the flaming rifles as they heralded the decrees of death during the entire war. Such examples of heroism, shown by both armies in that hand-to-hand struggle at Spottsylvania Court House, will not be lost to the Republic.

After the undecisive Battle of the Wilderness, Grant again tried to get his army between that of Lee and Richmond, and on the afternoon of May 7th began to move his army in the direction of Spottsylvania Court House. Lee had anticipated this movement on the part of Grant, and began at once to devise plans to throw his army across the path of his adversary. He therefore ordered General Anderson, who was now in command of Longstreet's corps, Longstreet having been wounded in the Battle of the Wilderness, to march by a shorter route to Spottsylvania Court House, hoping to reach the same before it was occupied by the troops of Grant. This movement was begun by Anderson on the night of May 7th. General Ewell was ordered to follow up Anderson's corps. This he did by taking a longer and more indirect route. When the Federals, under Warren, reached Todd's Tavern they found their cavalry in terrible conflict with Fitzhugh Lee's division of the Confederate cavalry. Fitzhugh Lee was reënforced by the advance division of Anderson's corps, which by this time had come up. General Warren was finally repulsed and fell back, thus giving the Confederates possession of Spottsylvania Court House which was gained only by the timely arrival of Anderson's corps.

The Federals tried again and again throughout the day to break the Confederate lines, but were repulsed in every attack. Thus Lee had again blocked the path of Grant.

Both armies began to entrench themselves, as it was very evident that a great battle was near at hand. The Confederates formed their entrenchments in the shape of a huge V, forming a salient angle against the center of the Federal line. This particular place has since been known as the "Bloody Angle." The Confederate left was commanded by Anderson, the center by Ewell, the right by Early, who was temporarily in command of A. P. Hill's corps, on account of Hill's sickness. The Federal left was commanded by Burnside, the center by Sedgwick and Warren, and the right by Hancock.

May 9th was spent by both armies in getting position and by some fighting between the outlying divisions of the armies. In one of these skirmishes General Sedgwick was killed by a sharpshooter's ball. He was succeeded in command by H. G. Wright. His death was a great loss to the Federal forces.

On the next day General Grant ordered a general attack on the Confederate line. This attack was led by General Warren, whose progress was very slow owing to the dense thickets of low cedar and the walls of abatis, which were thrown in their way by the Confederates. This advance of General Warren was met by a heavy artillery and musket fire from Longstreet's corps, under command of Anderson. Warren's troops came on notwithstanding the heavy fire from all sides. Some of his soldiers even crossed over the breastworks and were either killed or taken prisoners by the Confederates. The Federals finally retreated with heavy loss.

Grant now thought it best to attack the Confederate lines in front of Wright's corps. This was done late in the evening by several divisions under Upton. He advanced quickly through a terrible fire and gained the entrenchments, where they had a terrible hand-to-hand conflict with bayonets fixed. The Confederates were overpowered by numbers and gave way and fell back to their second line of entrenchments. For this brave act, Upton was made a brigadier-general. The Confederates, however, were reënforced, and Upton retired from the position which he had gained.

The battle was yet indecisive and both armies had suffered great loss. Owing to the heavy rains, the armies lay inactive on the 11th. It was during this battle that Grant sent a message to Washington saying that he would fight it out on this line if it took all summer.

Grant, in the meantime, had sent General Sheridan with his cavalry to threaten Richmond.

He was closely followed by General Stuart, and on May 11th they fought a hard battle at Yellow Tavern, in which General Stuart was killed. His death was a severe loss to the Confederacy. His experience as a cavalry leader, obtained on many battlefields, was such that his place could not be filled. A large statue has been erected to his memory in the Hollywood cemetery at Richmond, on which is recorded his feats of valor on many fields.

Grant decided on another attack on the Confederate lines at Spottsylvania on May 12th, the objective point being the sharp angle in Lee's entrenchments. This had been anticipated by General Lee, and he had been making ready. This attack was made at daybreak by General Hancock's corps. It was the most severe and the most bloody hand-to-hand conflict of the entire battle. The attack was received by General Johnston's brigade of Ewell's corps, which was finally overpowered and captured. This was the "Old Stonewall Brigade." This was a serious loss to Lee's army.

The Federals pushed on to the Confederates' second entrenchments, but were here repulsed by fresh troops under General Gordon. General Lee himself rode up with Gordon, but was forced back again by the cry of his own men: "General Lee to the rear!"

The fighting was kept up all day along the line. The trenches had to be cleared frequently of the dead to give room for the living. The slaughter continued until late in the night and was undecisive. The Confederates finally fell back within their entrenchments.

General Grant was deeply moved by the terrible loss of life at the "Bloody Angle."

The total loss to the Federals exceeded 18,000; the Confederates, about 9,000. Grant found that no ordinary methods of war would overcome the Army of Northern Virginia, and that his only hope was in the long drawn-out campaign with larger numbers. For the next five days short battles were fought at intervals between the outlying divisions of the armies.

Grant's army still moved to the southeast, with Lee following close along in their front, always ready to dispute any move that the Army of the Potomac should make toward Richmond.

THE BATTLE OF COLD HARBOR

With this battle terminated the Wilderness campaign, and was one over which Grant expressed regret, and said that Cold Harbor was the only battle that he ever fought that he would not fight over again, and he always regretted that the last assault at Cold Harbor was made.

The Federal commander had failed in his plan to pass around Lee to Richmond, and now saw that he must cross the James River and make Petersburg his objective point.

Early on the morning of May 26, 1864, Grant set his army in motion toward Cold Harbor. The next day Lee moved his army by a shorter route over the telegraph road to the Virginia Central railroad. The two armies were stretched across this low country parallel to each other and at times they came in contact.

On the 31st day of May, General Sheridan reached Cold Harbor. He had orders from Meade that he should hold this place at all hazards until the main army should arrive. Both armies had received reënforcements. The Confederates were reënforced by Breckinridge from western Virginia, and by Pickett from North Carolina. The Federals were reënforced from the army of General Butler from down the James River. Thus Grant's army was brought up to more than 100,000 men, and Lee's to about 75,000.

On May 31st Sheridan fought a severe battle with Fitzhugh Lee at Cold Harbor, but it was undecisive. On the next morning the Federal army arrived on the field and immediately took position. They were confronted by Longstreet's corps and that of A. P. Hill, and the divisions of Hoke and Breckinridge. Late in the evening the Federals made a fierce attack on the Confederate position and the Confederate lines were broken in many places, but before night they had succeeded in regaining some of their position.

It was well known to both armies that this battle would decide Grant's last chance to get between Lee and Richmond, and preparations were made the next day for a decisive battle on the morrow. The Federals were reënforced during the night of June 2d by Hancock's and Burnside's corps. The Confederates, being on the defensive, had orders from General Lee to rest on their arms and be ready to receive a fierce assault which he was anticipating from the Federals. It goes without saying that the Confederate soldiers under such orders on this particular night, and on account of the apparent danger of their position, did not close their eyes in sleep. The Federals were faced by Ewell's, A. P. Hill's and Longstreet's corps, the latter being under the command of Anderson, as Longstreet was severely wounded in the Battle of the Wilderness.

Both armies lay very close to each other, and Lee's position was exceptionally strong, as it must be approached through swampy ground, and his batteries were set in position to give both a front and an enfilading fire. Yet Grant determined to make a general attack on the Confederate lines, and passed word to his corps commanders to make ready to execute the same at about five o'clock on the morning of June 3d.

This order was carried out, and they had marshaled their soldiers in large numbers into lines ten columns deep, and at the appointed hour began with a determined step to move toward the Confederate entrenchments. The silence of the early morning was broken by the Confederate batteries and their musketry that raked the open country over which the Federals were advancing, which made the same appear as a fiery furnace. The columns of blue were swept by this fierce fire, which mowed them down in great numbers. They succeeded in crossing into the Confederate entrenchments in a few places and engaged in hand-to-hand combat, but the Confederates had orders to hold their position at all hazards, and the Federal leaders soon found it was impossible to stand the raking fire from the Confederate batteries and ordered a retreat, and in doing so they took with them a few hundred prisoners. Thus the field was left in the possession of the Confederates.

This battle is said to have lasted but twenty minutes, and during this short time Grant lost   10,000 men. This is said to be the greatest loss in the shortest time during the entire war.

With this battle ended the series of battles beginning with that of the Wilderness, all having been fought within a month, and nothing like it has yet been known to warfare.

Grant's entire loss in all these engagements in killed, wounded and missing was about 55,000 men, and that of the Confederates much less. If Lee's loss had been equal to that of Grant's, his army would have been almost annihilated.

DEDICATING THE NATIONAL CEMETERY AT GETTYSBURG

The soldiers, either living or dead, who stood in the dense columns of blue and marched across that shell swept field toward the Confederate entrenchments, and those who stood in the Confederate ranks and successfully repulsed that awful onslaught of the Federals on that bright June morning at Cold Harbor, for these reasons are possessed of a rich heritage which their posterity should be proud to receive.

SHERMAN'S MARCH TO THE SEA

General Sherman was given command of the Western army, which was to operate against Joseph E. Johnston, who was in command of the Confederate army in the West. Johnston was reckoned second to Lee in military genius. Sherman found under his command 120,000 men, while that of Johnston's army numbered about 75,000. The Federals were concentrated around Chattanooga, while the Confederates were massed at Dalton, where they had been in winter quarters.

Sherman moved his army on May 6, 1864, against Johnston, and thus the beginning of Sherman's march to the sea and a series of battles fought, viz.: Resaca, Kenesaw Mountain, Peach Tree Creek and the Battle of Atlanta.

Sherman's army was divided into three divisions commanded by Generals McPherson, Schofield and Thomas. His army was in good spirits and seemed anxious for the opportunity to move forward, after a long wearisome winter in camp, and rejoiced at the journey before them, though their mission was to be one of strife and bloodshed.

General Johnston had succeeded General Bragg in command of this Confederate army, which was now divided into two corps, commanded by Generals   Hood and Hardee. He was later reënforced by General Polk.

On account of the strong position occupied by Johnston at Dalton Sherman thought best to refrain from attacking him there and moved round to the right of the Confederate army to Resaca.

When Johnston discovered this movement on the part of the Federals he quickly evacuated Dalton and moved with all speed to Resaca, which place he succeeded in reaching before it was occupied by the Federals. On his way to Resaca his cavalry, under General Wheeler, fought a desperate battle with that of the Federals, under General McCook, in which Wheeler was successful.

The Confederates were strongly entrenched at Resaca by the time Sherman's army came up.

On May 14th Sherman ordered a general attack on the Confederate stronghold, which was done by Thomas' division and a part of

Schofield's. This attack was received by Hood's corps. There was desperate fighting and the advantage first lay with one and then the other, when at length the Federals were reënforced by General Hooker, and the Confederates fell back to the second line of their entrenchments.

There was terrible fighting on the next day during which the outworks were captured by General Butterfield, but he was unable to hold his position gained on account of the raking fire from Hardee's corps, which galled him very much.

During the night Johnston withdrew his army from Resaca toward Atlanta, and was closely followed by Sherman, who sent a part of his army under General Davis to capture Rome, a small town in Georgia, where there was quite a number of iron factories.

This he did, and destroyed the factories, which were a serious loss to the Confederates, for they were used for the manufacture of cannon and other munitions of war.

Johnston brought his army to a halt at Adairsville, at which place he had fully decided to give battle to Sherman, and had so informed his officers. After skirmishing with the enemy for some time he suddenly changed his mind and withdrew his army to Cassville, where he took a strong position and issued a spirited address to his army, and had fully decided to give battle to Sherman, but, on account of his superior numbers, Sherman had been able to turn the right flank of the Confederate army.

On the advice of Hood and Polk, Johnston again withdrew his army from its position and took a much stronger position a few miles south on Kenesaw Mountain.

On account of these several retreats, gave rise to a cause of a great deal of dissent among his soldiers, as well as the inhabitants of the country through which he passed, which left them in the hands of the enemy, but it is conceded that Johnston did the best he could, as his army was inferior to that of Sherman both in numbers and equipment, and he was waiting for an opportunity to catch Sherman's army divided, or to get a strong position which would help him in repulsing any attack made by Sherman. This strong position he found at Kenesaw Mountain, and here made ready for battle in earnest.

A few days prior to this, while Johnston's army was retiring from its former position at Cassville, they became engaged with a division of the Federal army at Pine Mountain, in which battle General Polk was killed by a cannon ball. This was a serious loss to the Confederacy. He was a graduate of West Point; but after being graduated he took work with the Episcopal church as bishop, but at the outbreak of the war he entered the Confederate army and served with distinction. Only a short time before his death it is reported that he administered the ordinance of baptism to Generals Johnston and Hood. It is said that he was rebuked by some of his church for taking up arms. He replied that he felt as a man plowing in a field and was called by his neighbor to help extinguish the flames from his house which was on fire, and after the fire would go back to work. He was succeeded in command by General Loring.

Sherman decided to attack Johnston at Kenesaw Mountain, this being anticipated by Johnston and, on account of his strong position, met with his approval. This desperate battle was fought on the 27th day of June. Sherman's army advanced against the strong Confederate works again and again during the day, but every charge was repulsed, the mountainside being swept by the musketry and artillery of the Confederates. Sherman's loss in this battle was more than 3,000 men, while that of the Confederates was less than 1,000.

Sherman was convinced that his success did not lay in attacking his antagonist in a strong position, and turned upon Johnston's right and attempted to pass around him to Atlanta in the same manner in which Grant was trying to pass around Lee to Richmond.

Sherman succeeded in drawing Johnston away from Kenesaw Mountain, and Johnston withdrew his army by shorter roads within the entrenchments before Atlanta, which was immediately confronted by the Federal hosts. This was a critical time for Sherman, as the North was in a presidential campaign in which it appeared that the success of the war party depended upon his capture of Atlanta; and on the other hand it was a critical time for the Confederates, for the loss of Atlanta would mean the loss of their iron foundries, where they manufactured most of their munitions of war, and besides would divide their country in two divisions again as Grant's capture of Vicksburg had divided it before.

General Johnston was removed from command of the army for the reasons assigned by the Confederate government that he had failed to arrest the advance of the enemy to the vicinity of Atlanta, and that he had expressed no confidence that he could defeat or repel Sherman, and for these reasons he was relieved and the same was handed to General Hood. It was said that when General Johnston received this information he informed General Hardee, who was with him, of the information received. Hardee replied, "I don't believe it." In answer Johnston said, "A thing may be unbelievable and a fact."

The removal of Johnston from the command is thought to have been a great mistake on the part of the Confederate Government, as his tactics had been in this campaign on the defensive on account of his inferior numbers and equipment to that of Sherman, while that of Hood was on the aggressive, and he maintained the idea of attacking Sherman's army, which proved to be the loss of Atlanta for the Confederacy.

Hood found himself in command of about 60,000 men, and on July 20th offered battle which was fierce and a decided loss to the Confederates, in which they were repulsed on every hand, but not without hard fighting and much loss to the Federals, for General Hood had the reputation of being a fearless, aggressive commander. This was known as the Battle of Peach Tree Creek.

Two days later, on July 22d, the Battle of Atlanta was fought, this being the greatest engagement of the entire campaign.

The Federals had closed in upon Atlanta and had succeeded in capturing some out entrenchments, but on the 22d was a general engagement of all the army, the attack being made by Hood to recapture some of his lost positions. In this engagement General McPherson was killed, which was a great blow to the Union army. General Logan succeeded to his command.

The Confederates achieved considerable success, but the Federals were presently reënforced, and Hood withdrew within the defenses of

Atlanta. Again on the 28th the Federals were attacked by General Hardee and a fierce battle was fought at Ezra Church, in which the Confederates were defeated with heavy loss.

Sherman determined on besieging the city and if possible destroy the line of supplies for Hood's army. This he succeeded in doing late in August by destroying the Macon and Western railroad.

Hood determined to attack the Federals and sent General Hardee to make an attack near Jonesboro, while he himself should attack Sherman's right flank. These attacks failed, thus necessitating the evacuation of Atlanta, which he did on September 2d, after destroying all the supplies he could not take with him.

Hood kept his army between that of Sherman's and Andersonville, at which place there were confined many thousands of Federal prisoners. With the fall of Atlanta practically ended the points of interest of Sherman's march to the sea.

The command of Hood's army was later given back to General Joseph E. Johnston.

BATTLE OF CLOYD MOUNTAIN

In the early spring of 1864 the command of the Union forces in the Shenandoah Valley was given to General Hunter, who made ready to march upon Lynchburg, with the object of taking possession of the city and to capture large stores of provisions and munitions of war which belonged to the Confederates and were stored at Lynchburg. He also laid waste to the country over which his army passed so as to render the same of little value as a source for supplies to the Confederacy.

A division of his army under General Crooks fought a desperate battle on the 9th day of May, 1864, with the Confederates, commanded by General Jenkins, at Cloyd's farm, near Dublin depot, in southwestern Virginia. This was one of the most severe short engagements of the entire war, in which General Jenkins was killed and the total loss to the Confederates in killed and wounded and missing was about 900, and that of the Federals somewhat less. During this short engagement the grim monster Death was on every side, and whose threatening shrieks howled in the air around them.

Hunter's main army finally reached the vicinity of Lynchburg on the 17th day of June, after fighting a battle with Imboden and Mc Causland a few miles away from Lynchburg, the Confederates falling back within the breastworks which they had hastily thrown up. The city was defended by a portion of Breckinridge's division, but their numbers were far inferior to that of the Federals, who had by this time arrived before the city. Hunter halted his army and brought up his artillery and did some cannonading, but went into camp with the expectation of taking the city without much opposition the next morning. It is thought that he could have easily taken the city on the evening of his arrival, but during the night General Gordon arrived with his division and the Confederates were reënforced by other arrivals next morning from the army of General Early, then on its way to the Shenandoah Valley. On the morning of the 18th General Hunter found Lynchburg full of Confederate soldiers, and more arriving on every train, which on the arrival the bands playing could plainly be heard by the Federal soldiers as they came upon the field. Hunter soon found, in his opinion, the capture of Lynchburg an impossibility, and his raid was to terminate in a dismal failure. During the 18th there was some cannonading and several skirmishes between the cavalry of the two contending armies.

On the night of the 19th he broke camp and marched away to the westward. Why he retreated without giving battle was not understood. General Gordon said that in his opinion that conscience was harrowing General Hunter and causing him to see an avenger wrapped in every gray jacket before him. The Confederates took up the pursuit of Hunter's retreating army, but Hunter succeeded in getting back across the mountains into western Virginia, after hard marches over mountain roads with little or no supplies for his army, and with a large amount of straggling.

General Lee dispatched General Early with an army of 20,000 men to threaten Washington, in the hope of drawing part of Grant's army away from before Richmond. Early was to go by the way of Shenandoah Valley. This route was given him partly in order to help defend Lynchburg and to get supplies for his army in the valley. He reached Winchester on the 3d of July, and moved rapidly down the valley and crossed into Maryland, and was at Hagerstown on the 6th. He turned about and moved boldly upon Washington. He met and defeated General Wallace on the Monocacy on July 9th, and on the next day he was within six miles of the capitol at Washington. An immediate assault might have given him possession of the city, which was weakly defended, but he delayed for a day, and in the meantime two divisions under General Wright from Grant's army from before Petersburg arrived and Early was forced to retreat, after spending the 12th in threatening the city. This was considered one of the boldest raids of the entire war.

This attack on Washington by General Early created considerable excitement in the city, for no other Confederate army had ever been so near to the capital before. The government employees of all kinds, the sailors from the navy yard, and the convalescents from the hospitals, were all rushed out to the forts around the city. Even President Lincoln himself went out to the defenses of the city.

Early recrossed the Potomac at Snickers' Ferry on the 18th. Here he was overtaken by the pursuing Federals, at which place a battle was fought in which Early was the victor. He fought another battle at Winchester with General Averell's cavalry.

Grant decided to give the command of the army in the Shenandoah to General Philip H. Sheridan, to whom he gave instructions to drive the Confederates out of the valley once for all, and to destroy all growing crops and everything that would be of any advantage to the Confederacy in the way of supplies for their army or otherwise. This he finally did, and Sheridan afterwards said that he believed a crow could fly over the entire valley without getting even a mouthful to eat.

September found the two armies near Winchester, and on the 19th a severe battle was fought which was kept up the entire day, the advantage being first with one side and then the other. Finally the Confederates, being outnumbered, retreated back through Winchester. This was a bloody day, in which the loss of the Federals was about 5,000, and that of the Confederates about 4,000.

The next day the Confederates were overtaken at Fisher's Hill, at which place Early was making preparations for a great battle, which engagement did not occur until the 22d. This engagement proved to be disastrous to Early, his army being flanked by the Federals with superior numbers. He began a stubborn retreat, which finally became a rout. He was closely followed up by the Federals, and fought several small engagements on his retreat.

On about the middle of October he received reënforcements from Longstreet, and on the 19th he attacked Sheridan's army at Cedar Creek, under the immediate command of General Wright, Sheridan having gone to Washington, but returned in time to take part in the battle. This took place about twenty miles from Winchester, the attack being made by General Gordon, who fell upon General Sheridan's men while they were yet sleeping early in the morning. Gordon was immediately supported by the army; Early himself came up to the attack. The Federals were completely surprised and retreated, which became a rout, leaving their entire camp equipment, together with some prisoners, in the hands of the Confederates. The Confederates thought they had gained a signal victory, and gave up the pursuit of the retreating Federals, and turned their attention to pillaging the Federal camp.

General Sheridan was on his way from Winchester to his army headquarters at Cedar Creek when he heard the roar of the cannon which convinced him that a great battle was being fought. He at once made haste to take charge of his army, this being Sheridan's famous ride. He first met stragglers of his army, and then passed through brigade after brigade of his retreating army, which so blocked the highway that he was compelled to leave the same and take to the fields. He at length succeeded in stopping the retreat and turned it into an attacking column. In this retreat were two divisions commanded by two future presidents, viz.: President Hayes and McKinley. This attack on the Confederates completely surprised them, and they were utterly routed and so badly defeated that Early's army was never completely reorganized, this being the last principal engagement in the Shenandoah Valley.

Previous to these battles in the valley, Early had dispatched General McCausland with his division of cavalry to go into Pennsylvania to levy large sums of money on the towns in reprisal for Hunter's depredations in the Shenandoah Valley. This cavalry party burned the town of Chambersburg.

THE SIEGE AND FALL OF PETERSBURG

After the battle of Cold Harbor Grant remained a few days trying to find a weak place in the Confederate lines. This he abandoned and resolved to move his army across the James and to Petersburg, which place is about twenty miles from Richmond, and was defended by General Beauregard with a small division of the Confederate army.

Petersburg was at the junction of three railroads, and was a place of great importance to the Confederacy, as all the supplies of Lee's army, as well as to Richmond, came by the way of Petersburg, and for these reasons General Grant resolved to destroy the railroads, and if possible to capture the city, and thus destroy the Confederates' source of supplies.

These conditions being well known to Lee, he resolved to defend Petersburg, and to save it from capture if possible, and thus began the greatest struggle of its kind known in modern times.

The advance divisions of Grant's army, under Hancock and W. F. Smith, appeared before Petersburg June 15, 1864. Beauregard managed to hold the entrenchments with his small force until Lee's main army arrived, which came by a shorter route than the one which the Federals had taken. Both armies were in full force before Petersburg by the evening of the 18th, and the great struggle had now begun. The Confederate entrenchments extended for thirty miles, and the whole country was a network of fortifications. Grant at once began to extend his lines of entrenchments, and thus the two armies were pitted against each other for their last great struggle, the army of General Grant numbering more than 100,000 men, while that of General Lee was about half that number.

General Grant turned his attention to trying to destroy the railroads, and made several attempts with much hard fighting to do so. But this, having been anticipated by General Lee, he had given to A. P. Hill the defense and the protection of the railroads, which was his source of supplies. They were ably protected by General Hill, and Grant's attacking parties in every instance were repulsed, and these plans were at length abandoned by him for the present.

The two armies lay facing each other before Petersburg the entire summer and fall, with several small engagements during the summer and a few very severe ones.

A severe cavalry engagement was fought at Trevilian Station, north of Richmond, on June 11th, between the Confederates, commanded by Generals Hampton and Fitzhugh Lee, and the Federals, commanded by General Sheridan.

During the latter days of July the Federals were engaged in digging a mammoth tunnel, beginning in the rear of their entrenchments and to extend under the Confederate fortifications before Petersburg, at the completion of which they expected to fill the same with large quantities of gunpowder which was to be exploded and was expected to blow up the Confederate fortifications.

Of all the schemes employed by either army this was the greatest, and one in which Grant had great faith, and the progress of which was watched with great anxiety. The Confederates were apprised of this undertaking, and had made ready by placing several batteries within their lines so that the fire from the same would sweep the opening which would be made by the blowing up of the "crater." At a few minutes past five on the morning of July 30th this mine was exploded, which was a sight to behold. The Federal troops who were in waiting to march through the opening were somewhat delayed from the shock and horror of the explosion, but at length marched in the opening in great numbers, and by this time the Confederate batteries were brought into action, which so horribly swept their ranks, and they were charged by General Mahone with several divisions of Georgia troops, and the Federal loss became so great, and their ranks in so much confusion, that they were ordered to retire within their entrenchments, thus bringing to a dismal failure the capture of Petersburg by this plan.

BATTLE OF SPOTTSYLVANIA COURT-HOUSE

During the last days of August Grant renewed his plan to destroy the Weldon railroad. This task was given to General Warren, with a large force who, after fighting several hard battles with the dashing Mahone, whose numbers were greatly inferior to that of Warren, and from his reputation for strategy it is thought that he was very worthy to wear the mantle of "Stonewall" Jackson, the Federals succeeded in destroying this railroad in several places.

Grant continued to extend his lines, and by the end of October he was very near the Southside railroad, and on the 27th fought a desperate battle with A. P. Hill at Hatcher's Run, in which the Federals were defeated and retired within their entrenchments before Petersburg, this being the last engagement of importance until the coming spring.

The suffering and privation endured by Lee's army during the winter of 1864 and 1865, while they lay within the defenses of Petersburg and Richmond with scant clothing and food, can scarcely be imagined by anyone excepting those who were there. Their numbers were depleted by sickness and other causes so by the coming of spring Lee had within his ranks less than 50,000 men.

Lee's lines had been extended until they were so thin that there was danger of breaking. A. P. Hill held the right, Gordon and Anderson the center, and Longstreet the left. Late in February Grant's army was reënforced by General Sheridan from the valley, and in the last days of March it was further reënforced from General Butler's army from down the James River.

General Lee began to see the position that he was in with his army against superior numbers and equipment, and felt that he must sooner or later evacuate Petersburg, and began to plan a junction of his army with General Johnston's in North Carolina.

General Grant anticipated this plan of Lee's and began to extend his lines westward so if possible to cut off Lee's chances of retreat.

Lee determined to make a bold attack on Grant's right, the objective point being Fort Stedman. This plan was given to General Gordon to be carried out, which he gallantly did, and captured the fort, but was unable to hold the same, and retired within the Confederate lines. His attack and capture of Fort Stedman was carefully planned and well supported by the main Confederate army.

The battle at Fort Stedman did not interfere with Grant's plan in extending his lines along the front of the Confederate army, under General Warren. Lee had sent General Anderson to hold the road over which he would retreat in the event he was compelled to evacuate Petersburg.

On the 31st a large Confederate force was at Dinwiddie Court House, and during that night they took a strong position at Five Forks, and here on April 1st a hard battle was fought, the Federals being commanded by Generals Sheridan and Warren. The Confederates were finally defeated with a loss of 5,000 prisoners.

The Confederates' defeat at Five Forks was a great blow to Lee, and he immediately began preparations for the evacuation of Petersburg and Richmond.

On the night of April 1st Grant began his attack all along his lines, which he kept up the entire night. His cannon threw shells into the doomed city, and at dawn on April 2d the assault began. The Federal troops went forward in an impetuous charge through a storm of grape and canister which was poured into their ranks. The Confederates fell back within their inner breastworks and the Federals pushed on the left as far as Hatcher's Run, where they had a severe engagement in which the Confederate General Pegram was killed, and another engagement near the Southside railroad in which General A. P. Hill was killed. His death was an irreparable loss to the Confederacy. He was one of their able corps commanders, and had been in all the principal engagements in the East. He played a distinctive part in the Seven Days' Battles before Richmond; his timely arrival on the field saved Lee's army from utter rout at Antietam Creek and turned defeat into partial victory; he was a great favorite of "Stonewall" Jackson, and took a distinctive part in the battles of Fredericksburg and Chancellorsville, in which last-named battle he was near by when "Stonewall" Jackson was mortally wounded; with his corps was first on the field at Gettysburg; his corps received the first onslaught of the Federals at the Battle of the Wilderness; was too sick to command his corps at Spottsylvania Court House, which was temporarily commanded by General Early; played a distinctive part at Cold Harbor, and here at Petersburg, on Sunday, April 2d, the end. He was buried in the cemetery at Petersburg on the night of April 2d, while the whole country was being lit up by bursting shells and the hurrying and noise of the progress of a great battle.

On Sunday morning, April 2d, General Lee notified the authorities at Richmond that he must evacuate Petersburg at once, and to notify President Davis of the situation. President Davis was at St. Paul's Church with several of his cabinet listening to a sermon by Dr. Minnegerode, speaking of a supper before Gethsemane. The sexton walked up the isle and handed the President the message, which he read, and quietly retired from the church, this being noticeable on account of it being somewhat out of the ordinary, although they were accustomed to the roar of the cannon at Petersburg. However, it was soon known that Petersburg and Richmond were soon to be evacuated, and the service was dismissed at the church without further announcement.

The city of Richmond was in a state of excitement as the officers of the government departed from the city on their way to Danville, and during the night the arsenals were set on fire by the evacuating troops. The flames spread to a large portion of the city, which was burned. The next day the city was taken charge of by the Federals.

THE SURRENDER AT APPOMATTOX

We are now to the closing scenes of the greatest civil war of modern times.

Lee evacuated Petersburg early on the third morning of April, 1865, and retreated toward Amelia Court House.

With the evacuation of Petersburg also fell the city of Richmond. For nine months Lee's invincible forces had kept a foe more than twice their numbers from invading their capital.

Lee had ordered supplies for his army to Amelia Court House, for which they were in sore need, as they had been on little or no rations for several days, but by some mistake of orders the train of supplies had been sent on to Richmond. This serious mistake was a crushing blow to Lee's army, for when his troops reached Amelia Court House and found no supplies, which had been promised them, their hopes sank within them. Lee, as well as his officers, had come to realize that the end of the great war could not be far distant.

Grant's army was hastening in pursuit of that of Lee's, Grant had sent General Sheridan to flank around Lee's army and get in his front, so if possible to cut off his chance of escape.

Lee had intended to concentrate his forces at Amelia Court House, but his whole army did not come up until the evening of the 5th, and on the discovery of his inadequate supplies he began the march anew toward Farmville, dividing his army so as to secure supplies from the country over which he passed. In the afternoon of April 6th Lee's army was overtaken by the Federals and a hard battle was fought at Sailor's Creek, in which General Richard Ewell, who was on the rear of Lee's army, was captured with his entire corps, numbering about 6,000 men.

Lee's main army reached Farmville on the night of the 6th of April, where they received their first rations within two days, and near which place a hard battle was fought, in which the Confederates, under General Mahone, gained a temporary victory.

The retreat was again renewed in the hope of breaking through the Federal lines, which were rapidly enveloping around them. During these marches the soldiers were so worn out from hunger, fatigue, and lack of sufficient clothing in the early spring weather, that there was much straggling from the army, and many had thrown their arms away until scarcely one-third of Lee's army was equipped for battle.

Lee's army reached Appomattox Court House late in the evening of April 8th, and here found the Federals in their front, and were compelled to stop and prepare for battle. General Lee and his officers held a council of war that night and decided to make a desperate effort to cut through the Federal lines the next morning. This task was assigned to General Gordon.

On Sunday, the 9th, Gordon made a fierce attack upon the Federals in his front, but was finally repulsed by overwhelming numbers, and sent word to General Lee that he could do nothing further unless he was heavily supported from Longstreet's corps.

With the repulse of Gordon on that morning sank Lee's last hope of breaking through the Federal lines, and he said there is nothing to do but see Grant.

Grant had proposed to Lee at Farmville, on the evening of the 7th, terms for the surrender of Lee's army, to which Lee replied that as much as he desired peace, yet the time certainly had not arrived for the surrender of the Army of Northern Virginia.

After the repulse of Gordon, on April 9th, Lee soon arranged a meeting with Grant and a truce was ordered pending negotiations for the surrender of Lee's army. This meeting took place at the house of Wilmer McLean at Appomattox Court House, at which place the terms were finally agreed upon by the two world famous commanders and were put in writing in the form of a letter from General Grant to General Lee, and the acceptance of the terms were written by Lee to Grant in the same form.

It is interesting to know that Wilmer McLean had lived on the battlefield of Bull Run during the progress of the first battle fought there, and after the battle moved to Appomattox Court House, and at his house was negotiated the terms of the surrender of Lee's army, thus around his premises was fought the first and the last great battle of the war.

The Confederate officers were allowed to retain their side arms, and the Confederate soldiers to retain their horses. This was a welcome concession.

Lee's army numbered less than 28,000 men, which he surrendered. Of these less than one-third were bearing arms on the day of surrender.

The Confederate soldiers for some time did not realize that negotiations for their surrender was on and were expecting and seemed to be anxious for another battle with General Sheridan in their front, and were greatly surprised on learning of the negotiations that had been completed for their surrender.

It was at once apparent to all that the great war was practically ended.

On the next day the surrender of the army was completed, and when Lee made his farewell address to his soldiers, who had so faithfully defended their faith in the Confederacy in all the hard battles in which they had been engaged, and especially since the Wilderness campaign, and in the defense of Petersburg and Richmond in the closing days, where their endurance was the greatest, and had now come down to the closing scenes at Appomattox, they were all deeply moved. General Lee, in broken accents, admonished them to be as brave citizens as they had been soldiers.

Thus practically ended the greatest civil war in history. Soon after Lee's surrender the other Confederate forces arranged for their surrender in quick succession.

It had been a long, bloody and devastating war, and it is said that there were more Confederate prisoners at Point Lookout alone than the number with Lee's army at the surrender.

The war closed on a spectacle of ruin the greatest yet known in America. While the smoke had cleared away, and the roar of the cannon had ceased, yet there could be heard the wailing of mothers, widows and orphans throughout both North and South, which is the greatest costs of so great and devastating war.

The Southern states lay prostrate; their resources gone; their fields desolate; their cities ruined; the fruits of the toil of generations all swept to destruction.

The total number of Union soldiers engaged were about a million and a half. Of this number, 275,000 were either killed in battle, died of mortal wounds or from disease in camp, and the loss to the Confederates was approximately the same. In both armies about 400,000 were disabled for life, thus making a grand total loss of about a million able-bodied men to the country.

At the close of the war over 60,000 Confederate prisoners were released. The records of the war department shows that 220,000 Confederates were made prisoners in the war. This includes, of course, the surrender of the armies at the close. Of this number 25,000 died of wounds and disease during their captivity. The estimated number of Union captives were about 200,000, of whom 40,000 died in captivity.

THE END

Made in the USA
Monee, IL
14 April 2026